OZZY

KNOWS

BEST

ALSO BY CHRIS NICKSON

Denzel Washington

Ewan McGregor

Lauryn Hill

Mariah Carey

Mariah Carey Revisited

Melissa Etheridge

Soundgarden

Will Smith

*Superhero: A Biography of
Christopher Reeve*

OZZY

Thomas Dunne Books

St. Martin's Griffin ❧ New York

KNOWS BEST

an

unauthorized

biography

chris nickson

the amazing story

of ozzy osbourne—

from heavy metal

madness to

father of the year

on mtv's *the*

osbournes

THOMAS DUNNE BOOKS.
An imprint of St. Martin's Press.

OZZY KNOWS BEST. Copyright © 2002 by Chris Nickson. All rights reserved. Printed in the
United States of America. No part of this book may be used or reproduced in any
manner whatsoever without written permission except in the case of brief quotations
embodied in critical articles or reviews. For information, address St. Martin's Press,
175 Fifth Avenue, New York, N.Y. 10010.

www.stmartins.com

ISBN 0-312-31141-9

First Edition: July 2002

10   9   8   7   6   5   4   3   2   1

For Raymond Ewart Nickson

November 2, 1914–January 20, 2001

Bad language isn't second nature to me, it's first.

Bad language and bad behavior.

It's a f***ing winning combination, you've got to admit.

—Ozzy Osbourne

OZZY

KNOWS

BEST

Introduction

No one expected this. Even with the wave of reality shows that have invaded popular culture, who'd have thought that a fly-on-the-wall show about an aging heavy metal superstar and his family would find a mass audience?

But that's exactly what happened.

Just a few weeks into its ten-week run, *The Osbournes* became a hit. Then a bigger hit. Then it became, to the network's—and the Osbournes'—astonishment, the biggest show in MTV's twenty-one-year history. And now it's the top-rated show on cable television, and episode seven, aired April 16, became the sixth most-watched show on television that night. And now it's also spread its wings to Canada and the U.K.

There's something going on here. When fifty-three-year-old Ozzy Osbourne, a man in the fourth decade of his musical career, can beat out Britney and the boy bands, the rappers and the wannabes in MTV's popularity stakes, life has taken a left turn.

MTV calls it a "reality sitcom." That's a nice catchphrase to hang on a series, but it's not true. A situation comedy is scripted. *The Osbournes* is anything but written; that's why almost every third word has to be bleeped out. As Ozzy notes, "As you see it is as it was." No careful edits, setups, camera angles, or makeup.

What it does have, in between the swearing, the throwing of hams over fences, and Ozzy's fetish for the History Channel, is a lot of love. You can see it between Ozzy and his wife of twenty years, Sharon. And they have it for their kids, Kelly, Jack, and Aimee (who decided not to be a part of the show), and also their brood of animals. And how much real love is there on television these days? For all the talk of family values that's been batted around these days, it's ironic that it should be a singer—who's probably best remembered for biting the head off a bat—who's teaching America about parenting.

And let's face it, for any couple to stay together twenty years these days is an achievement. To be fair, there was a brief separation (after Ozzy tried to strangle Sharon in 1989) but it was only while he was in rehab. After that, they were reconciled (and the charges against him were dropped). For a couple to successfully raise three children together is an even greater achievement. Through thick and thin, the Osbournes have always been there for each other.

But why did they decide to do the show? It certainly wasn't for the money. The $20,000 they've reportedly been paid for each episode is hardly going to make them rich, and besides, Ozzy's fortune is supposed to be around $58 million. Sharon, who's also been Ozzy's manager since 1982—the year they married—has to be a wealthy woman in her own right.

According to Ozzy, it was Sharon's idea ("Sharon is my boss, you know"). But it was an idea that had been around for a couple of years before it hit the screens. Back in early 2000, according to Erik Hedegaard in *Rolling Stone,* the Osbournes had met with a TV executive to discuss a sitcom that could possibly star the family, based on their everyday lives, although it would have been less than factual.

It didn't happen, but a little later, son Jack, sixteen, suggested the fly-on-the-wall concept, documenting their lives as they happened.

It would probably all have come to nothing if they hadn't been featured on MTV's show *Cribs* in July 2001. Going into the homes of different stars from all walks of music, *Cribs* proved to be unexpectedly popular, and the family Osbourne, so natural—and to some, so messed-up—was a huge success. Big enough for Sharon to resurrect Jack's concept. And for MTV to say yes. And by a perfect stroke of fate, filming could begin just as they were moving into a new house in Beverly Hills—the twenty-fourth place they'd lived.

In many ways, you can blame, or praise, MTV for the fact that reality television exists at all. They effectively began it with *The Real World,* which crammed a bunch of strangers together and filmed the results. It was a hit, but an isolated one. A few years elapsed before shows like *Big Brother* and *Survivor* became the temporary saviors of network television ratings.

But where all those dealt with anger, angst, and divisiveness, *The Osbournes* is warm and fuzzy. Even though daughter Aimee, now eighteen and trying to start her own singing career, wanted nothing to do with the show, no one's going to vote her out of the family—although she did opt to live in a separate building on the grounds for the four months during which filming was happening.

With its unanticipated popularity, the show has had two remarkable effects. It's brought an audience of people over the age of thirty-five to MTV. People who wouldn't know or care if they saw a Limp Bizkit or P.O.D. video have been tuning in every week by millions to catch up on what's been happening to Ozzy, Sharon, Jack, and Kelly (not to mention Lola and the other dogs, a nanny, and a bodyguard).

And it's brought Ozzy a whole new, younger audience. The man might have sold 70 million albums during his career, and influenced one, if not two, generations of musicians, from Soundgarden to Marilyn Manson. But his core group of fans, however large, had been aging, even when he'd been touring supported by younger acts in his annual Ozzfest. Now, all of a sudden, Ozzy Osbourne is a very real, and incredibly entertaining, father figure to a huge group of teens and twentysomethings. Who are now buying his albums, discovering his music, and snapping up tickets for this year's Ozzfest trek at a rapid rate so they can see the great man himself.

Suddenly everything's coming up Ozzy. The trickle-down effect is rapidly becoming a torrent. A quick glance at eBay, the online auction site, shows that the price for anything Osbourne-related, especially if autographed, is going through the roof.

"I was outbid the other day trying to get a signed '74 tour book," Mitch Van Beekum, Web master of the fan site www.ozzyhead.com, told Robin Platts in *Discoveries*. A copy of Ozzy's 1985 biography—unsigned—went for $31.

The bottom line is that Ozzy has a winning way. He might seem to be mentally absent at least some of the time, and confused by his family a lot more of the time, but he loves them all, even when they baffle him.

"I love you all," he told them. "I love you more than life itself. But you're all f***ing mad."

And that's what it's all about. Sticking together. His kids might exasperate him at times, such as when Kelly got a tattoo without permission (a tasteful little heart on her hip), but he's never going to turn his back on them. He cares in the way that every parent wants to care. He just expresses it differently, with a lot of four-letter words. You can call the Osbournes the family that puts the fun in dysfunctional, and maybe you'd be right, but there's more to it than that.

"Through all the craziness, you see that there's a family that loves each other and are really close," Sharon Osbourne explained. "I think that today, and especially in this industry, to find a family that wants to spend time together is unusual."

Which is why America has taken them to their hearts. They care about each other. And it's why Ozzy—a British heavy metal singer who occasionally used to bite the heads off small animals, who's been in rehab several times, and whose arms and knuckles are covered in tattoos—is in line to be America's Father of the Year.

He's Ozzy, not Ozzie, and the Osbournes most definitely aren't the Nelsons of *Ozzie and Harriet*. Or the Cunninghams of *Happy Days,* or even the sensitive, sweater-wearing Cosbys who formed the ideal of the nuclear family in the 1980s. They're not your normal family—but, underneath, which family really is?

Okay, not everyone will find themselves unpacking boxes marked "devil heads" and "dead things" alongside the linens and pots and pans when they move into a new home. But in Ozzy's case it comes with the territory. You can't make your mark singing about the Devil as part of Black Sabbath without picking up a few souvenirs. But at heart, this is a man who'd rather spend time on the couch with his son watching the History Channel, at least if he can figure out how to work the remote (luckily, Jack understands it).

Ozzy understands the impulses of teenagers. Maybe it's a while since he was one himself, but the rock'n'roll lifestyle has kept him young at heart. Over thirty years on the road, entertaining crowds in arenas around the world, have kept him in touch with his inner child. And that helps him communicate with his own kids. He's willing to listen. Sure, he'll lay down the law at times—all parents have to establish boundaries for their children, especially during the teen years, when they're continually testing limits. But how many can parent by example?

For instance, when Jack admitted to his father that he'd smoked pot, Ozzy didn't lose his temper, the way so many would have done. He didn't ground his son, which would be the immediate response of many. How could he? He'd been there. Instead, he could parent by example.

"It ain't gonna lead to anywhere but bad places," he explained to Jack. "Look at me."

Funny? Maybe. Effective? Without a doubt. But think about it for a minute. How many teens would feel comfortable enough to tell their parents they used drugs of any kinds? The statistics show that plenty of kids try pot at least once, and a number of them smoke it regularly. But would many of them sit down with their parents and tell them? Probably not.

And in that incident lies the magic the Osbournes share with each other. They're open with each other. Some might say a little too open at times. And because of that, they can discuss subjects all too often taboo in other families. The lines of communication—about anything—remain open.

Take away the long hair, the platinum records on the wall, and they're the same as every other family in America.

"We have the same problems as anybody else," Sharon sharply pointed out. "It's all relative, whether you're in the public eye or not, whether you have money or don't. You still have to deal with your kids and the issues of smoking pot and doing homework."

They just manage it all a little better than most, and we love them for it. Kids love them because they see parents who are cool, who they'd choose for themselves if they could (although the fact that the parents are rich in this case probably doesn't hurt, either). Parents relate to a couple coping very well with problems they recognize from their own lives.

And, at the core, is the love Ozzy and Sharon have for each other. While he can say that "Sharon and I have had some monumental arguments. It hasn't always been a bed of roses, believe me," they're a couple who can be found snogging backstage—much to the disgust of their kids—while waiting to be the guests of Jay Leno. It's sweet, it's touching, and it's the kind of relationship every couple would want, but few really manage, especially after having three children.

Really, there aren't any secrets to it. What you see on *The Osbournes* is what you get. Two parents and two kids with the usual dynamics and tension, underlaid by a whole lot of love. And with Ozzy as the unlikely, but very real, great father.

By rights, it probably shouldn't make great television, especially on youth-oriented MTV. But it has, and the viewing numbers keep growing week by week. With ten episodes in the season, each repeated a number of times during the week, and the opportunities for reruns and *The Osbournes* marathons during the summer, MTV has a big winner on its hands.

Negotiations are already under way for a second season, something that promises more joy to millions, and the show will undoubtedly be aired overseas: Thanks to the Internet, it already has global anticipation. And certainly the Osbourne family will see a lot more money for new episodes.

But there are other tie-ins, too. There'll be a soundtrack CD, already in the works, with Jack as producer, and Kelly making her singing debut, covering Madonna's "Papa Don't Preach," a slight irony, considering that her papa doesn't do a whole lot of preaching. This, after all, is the man who told her it was her decision whether or not to see the "vagina doctor," as he called her gynecologist.

And the album will be a hit. Why? Because we can't get enough of the Osbournes.

"Watching the Osbournes, you watch your own family," noted

former *Happy Days* star and family man Henry Winkler, and it's true. For all politicians and others who trumpet "family values" as being part of America, in the bustle of modern life we've lost touch with what makes a family a family.

But somehow or other, the Osbournes haven't. They have a closeness we envy. We want it for ourselves, even if the only way we can get it in the short-term is by watching them every week on television. Yes, they're funny, and often outrageous, as much the Addams family as the Cunninghams (but the Addams family were very close too) at times. But deep down we know we can learn from them.

And, let's face it, they're fun. How many times do you get to see a rock star take out his own trash or sit doodling at the kitchen table? How many wives have wanted to throw hams and cat shit at the neighbors, but never have because it wouldn't look good? The Osbournes keep the lid off, and in its own way, it's very healthy. They're the people we want to be, and hope to be.

Ultimately, it raises a question: Just who are the dysfunctional ones—them or us? Maybe it just depends which side of the fence you're on—throwing the hams, or having them thrown at you.

But one thing simply can't be denied. They're great parents, and Ozzy is a truly brilliant dad. How does he do it? And how does he make it seem so natural and, well, simple?

The lessons are in his own past. He's lived, and he's learned as he's gone along. Maybe we can't all be Ozzy—and maybe many wouldn't want to be—but we can still learn from him, and make our own lives better and richer.

"I'm just Dad," he said. And maybe he is. But he does it so f***ing well.

OZZY KNOWS BEST

TOP TELEVISION FATHERS

Ozzie Nelson

Jim Anderson

Ward Cleaver

Howard Cunningham

Mike Brady

Cliff Huxtable

Gomez Addams

Doggie Daddy

Ozzy Osbourne

TOP TELEVISION MOTHERS

Samantha Stevens

June Cleaver

Carol Brady

Shirley Partridge

Marian Cunningham

Clair Huxtable

Ann Romano

The Ozzman Cometh

It's never been easy to be Ozzy.

There have been the good times—plenty of them—and the bad times—plenty of those, too. Court cases and times in rehab have formed many of the lows, along with occasional swells of bad publicity. But they're all in the past, and the voice of heavy metal has come out the other side.

Right from the beginning it was rough. In the years after World War II, England was a bleak, austere place. Even though they'd won the war, food rationing was still in effect, and everything else seemed in short supply, too. Where German bombs had fallen, there were still often craters and rubble.

That was the world John Michael Osbourne was born into on December 3, 1948. Around him was Aston, part of the industrial city of Birmingham in the English Midlands. It wasn't pretty. A working-class area, it was made up of row houses whose bricks had been blackened over the years by pollution. Fourteen Lodge Road was no different from any of the other houses around it. That was where John Thomas Osbourne and his wife Lillian lived, and young John, the Ozzy to be, grew up with his five brothers and sisters—Paul, Tony, Jean, Iris, and Gillian.

John Sr. was a machinist. He had steady, skilled work on the night shift, but the money wasn't that good. Lillian, too, worked a full-time day shift for Lucas, who made car parts and accessories. With six kids to feed, it seemed there was never enough of anything to go around, be it food, clothes, or any kind of luxury. It made for a lot of tension.

"You hear your mother crying because she has no dough to feed you," Ozzy would remember, years later. "Or my father and her always fighting over something. And I used to sit on the front steps all the time and think, 'One of these days I'm going to buy a Rolls Royce and drive them out of this s***hole'. And I did it."

But while all the kids shared one bed in the tiny two-up, two-down house, which had a toilet outside in the tiny, concrete backyard, there was one escape—television. Somehow the Osbournes had scraped together enough to afford one of the sets, and young John was able to vanish into American programs like *I Love Lucy, Lassie,* and *Roy Rogers,* along with homegrown fare, such as *Robin Hood.*

At school, John quickly picked up a couple of nicknames, both from his surname. For a while it was "Oz-brain," which soon became just Ozzy—a name so familiar now that if someone calls him John, he doesn't even respond.

As students go, Ozzy wasn't the best. About the only thing he did love was music, at least after he—and the rest of England—discovered the Beatles. That changed his life. Before that, he said, his ambition was "to become a plumber. When I heard the Beatles I wanted to become a Beatle."

He and millions of other boys wanted exactly the same thing— the fame and the fortune. Some, like his classmate, Tony Iommi, learned to play guitar. Ozzy just sang. Back then, though, no one was listening, not even Iommi, who used to make fun of Ozzy's voice, calling it high and girly. Which perhaps it was, in the Gilbert and Sullivan operettas Ozzy was a part of at school, taking roles in *The Pirates of Penzance, H.M.S. Pinafore,* and *The Mikado.* It was a long way from "Paranoid," but at least he was up on a stage. And he was making people happy, which he'd always tried to do as a boy.

"When I was a child at school, if people were miserable around me, I'd do some crazy things like jump through f***ing doorways, anything to make them amused—hang myself, anything, because I hate to see sad faces."

Maybe Ozzy could have stayed in school. But he didn't want to. The constant arguments about money at home made him believe that if he brought home a wage, things might be better between his parents. So when he was fifteen, the lowest legal age to leave school, he quit, and began to try and fulfill his first ambition.

You start a career at the bottom, and Ozzy—as everyone called him now—was no exception. To learn the trade of a plumber, you started in the lowly job of plumber's mate—handing over tools, making tea, and hopefully being shown how to do things. The pay was bad, and the work was worse.

After a few months he'd had enough. Anything was better than this. At least, Ozzy thought so. And by the 1960s, with England starting to swing, and the economy booming, there were plenty of jobs, even for a kid with absolutely no qualifications. So Ozzy found employment in a slaughterhouse, where he found himself killing cattle and cutting out sheep guts.

It was a long way removed from glamour and the fashionable King's Road in London. And it wasn't going to make him rich. It wasn't even going to make him comfortable.

So he moved on again, joining his mother at the Lucas plant, where his job was tuning car horns. It had its appeal for a short while, but it would never be his favorite musical job. As he said later, "I liked heavy metal better because it was louder." He worked, he remembered, in "a soundproof booth. These f***ing car horns are coming down a conveyor belt, and you're in this f***ing chamber—a box, like something out of f***ing Flash Gordon. You take a car horn, put it in this clamp, and you tune this f***ing thing in to the dial."

From there it was on to a series of other jobs, including a short stint at a crematorium—possibly the ideal training ground for a heavy metal icon who's long been associated (quite wrongly) with the Dark Side.

But wherever he went, the money was terrible and the prospects seemed nonexistent. And the chances of him suddenly becoming a Beatle were slim. If he was going to get ahead fast, there seemed to be only one answer—a life of crime.

The way to do it, he thought, was burglary—some sneaky breaking and entering when no one was home. He'd seen enough television to know that if you wore gloves, you didn't leave fingerprints. However, that only worked if the gloves you wore had fingers. Ozzy put on a pair of fingerless gloves for his first bite out of a life of crime.

Unsurprisingly, with clues left all over the place, Ozzy was nabbed by the long arm of the law, and made his first court appearance. He got off lightly, having been given a fine. But without a job, he had no money to pay it, and ended up in jail for three months.

It should have been the short, sharp shock to send him scurrying back to the straight and narrow. Instead it became the scene of Ozzy's first artwork, with himself as the canvas. Using a sewing needle and powdered graphite—a method he definitely wouldn't recommend these days—he made his first tattoos. On the knuckles of one hand he inscribed OZZY. The palm of the other hand had the word THANKS. And on each knee he etched a smiley face; he did those, he claimed, so he'd see something happy when he woke up each morning.

Released, but now with a prison record, he decided he'd learned from his mistake. Next time he'd be more careful. And he was, getting away with a television set. But in those days TVs were bulky, heavy items, awkward to handle alone, something Ozzy quickly discovered.

Poised on top of a wall, trying to balance himself and the set, he fell. So did the TV—right on top of him. Which the way the police discovered Ozzy a little while later. That landed him in Birmingham's Winson Green prison for two months. And it wasn't the last time young Ozzy would end up behind bars. No sooner had he gotten out than he was back inside for punching a police officer in the face.

HOW TO BE AN OZZY PARENT:

Tell your kids not to do the crime if they can't do the time. They have to learn to be responsible for their own actions.

It was 1967, and flower power was in the air. The Beatles were the biggest group in the world. Pop stars were being treated like royalty, all over the papers with money to burn. Out of jail again, an eighteen-year-old Ozzy knew two things—he didn't want to see the inside of a cell again, and he wanted to break into music.

But with no job and no contacts, it didn't look as though success was going to be tapping him on the shoulder anytime soon. But just like becoming a plumber, rock'n'roll required an apprenticeship.

The first stage happened when Ozzy, still jobless, was walking around the Birmingham streets. He ran into a friend he'd known at school, who announced he'd started a band called Approach. All they lacked was a singer.

And that was easily remedied.

Ozzy could sing. And he wanted in.

There was only one problem. He didn't have an amplifier or a microphone for his voice, which he needed to be heard above the electric guitars and drums. Nor did he have any money to buy one.

But his father did.

It was probably a surprise to Ozzy when his father agreed to spend $50—hard-earned money in those days—to buy his son the equipment he needed for his new career. But he happily accepted the gift. Oz was set and ready to become a star.

At least until he began playing with the band. Approach, as he quickly discovered, was a soul band. But even then Ozzy Osbourne wasn't a soul singer, by any stretch of the imagination. So they quickly parted ways. Then there was a short stint in a band called Music Machine, who rapidly went nowhere.

Frustrated, yet still determined to make his mark in music, Ozzy—who was now calling himself Ozzy Zig—decided to follow the time-honored route for finding other musicians to play with, by placing an ad in a music shop.

OZZY ZIG—VOCALIST—REQUIRES BAND—OWNS OWN P.A.

With a microphone and amp, he was maybe stretching the truth a little on the P.A. system, but it was still more than most amateur singers had. The ad did bring results, though. Ozzy was contacted by another guy his age, Terrence Butler, known to everyone as Geezer. He'd been playing guitar for six months, and he was eager to start a band.

So that was what he and Ozzy did, starting their own band and naming it Rare Breed.

Like so many groups, Rare Breed died quickly, after just two shows. But Ozzy and Geezer had become friends. They knew they had something, even if they didn't know what it was.

Meanwhile, Tony Iommi, who just a few years before had mocked Ozzy's voice, was also trying to make his living from music. So far he'd done better than Ozzy. He'd teamed up with drummer William Ward—Bill to his mates—a lorry driver's assistant, and together they'd formed a group called the Rest, along with a singer named Chris Smith. A blues band, they'd moved north to Carlisle—near the Scottish border—and established themselves on the local circuit after changing their name to the more ambiguous Mythology.

All good things come to an end, and Mythology ground to a halt. When it was over, Tony and Bill made their way back to the familiar ground of Birmingham, where Iommi spotted Ozzy's notice in the music store, and just hoped it wasn't the same kid he'd known at school, who sang like a girl.

Of course it was.

And to make matters worse, Ozzy had short hair, which wasn't good for a band's image at the time.

He wasn't cool.

Needless to say, their meeting didn't go well.

Still, that didn't stop Ozzy and Geezer from turning up at Tony's house a few days later. They needed a drummer, and hoped Tony might know of one. As it turned out, Bill was there, and he agreed to join their group. There was one condition—Tony had to be a part of it, too.

So it was Ozzy, Geezer, Tony, and Bill.

And, it turned out, there was a slide guitar player and a saxophonist, too, not exactly a lineup of metal legend. But that wasn't the intention when they came together. Instead, they headed back to Carlisle, where Mythology had been big, and tried to pick up where the earlier band had left off, a piece of some local fame, along with some money.

It didn't work. They disbanded, which turned out to be a ruse simply to get rid of the slide player and saxist. Then they reformed, calling themselves the Polka Tulk Blues Band (according to legend, the name came from a tin of talcum powder Ozzy found in a dustbin), that quickly changed to Earth, and Butler moved to bass. Since he couldn't actually afford a real bass guitar, he took off the top two strings of his six-string, and retuned it.

"The stuff we had when we first started was all twelve-bar blues," recalled Geezer Butler. "We used to do a lot of Willie Dixon songs, Howlin' Wolf, Lightnin' Hopkins, and Muddy Waters. We learned them from listening to the records. They were easy to play. When we first came together we formed in one day and had a gig a week later. We never had played together so we learned eighteen twelve-bar blues numbers in a week." But with just three chords and a lot of repetition, that wasn't difficult.

Although Ozzy was the front man, he didn't always have a lot to do. In the style of the day, Earth jammed a lot onstage. As Tony Iommi said, "it was mainly instrumental. We'd do a bit of vocals and then ten minutes of instrumental. It was good for us to do that."

They'd started. But it was still a hard row to hoe. What they needed next was somewhere to play, and that proved to be a Birmingham venue called Henry's Blues House, located in the center of town. It was owned by Jim Simpson, a jazz musician, and the band not only approached him for a gig at the club, but also to manage them. He gave them a big break, a slot opening for Ten Years After, then one of the big underground blues-rock bands.

"Ten Years After was one of our heroes," Iommi recalled. "Alvin Lee was billed as 'the fastest guitar in Britain.' One of our big breaks was when we did a gig with him. We supported Ten Years After and they really liked what we were doing. Alvin Lee got us a gig at the Marquee in London. That sort of started the ball rolling for us."

Simpson began managing them, but it couldn't be said that he was a major fan.

"Ozzy had no technical qualifications really," he said. "At least Tony or Geezer could play their scales or a B flat chord. Ozzy wouldn't know what a chord was if it fell out of the sky and hit him on the head. He knew nothing about music whatsoever. All he had was feel. But he had far more going for him than the rest of the band. The band, in my opinion, was purely Ozzy."

For a couple of weeks, however, the band almost wasn't anything, as Tony Iommi was recruited by another young band, Jethro Tull, to fill the guitar slot left open by the departure of Mick Abrahams. He even made one appearance with them, on the Rolling Stones' *Rock and Roll Circus,* although it took around three decades for it to appear.

But he returned quickly, and the band continued playing Henry's Blues House—supposedly recording a jazzy demo for their manager called "Song for Jim," their first time in a studio. At least that was what they thought until some fans turned up and said they liked their new single. That came as a surprise, since as far as the band knew, they didn't have a single.

Another band called Earth did, however, and that meant a name change was in order. They'd seen a poster for a Boris Karloff movie called *Black Sabbath,* and decided to use that (Geezer's interest in the occult through the black magic novels of Dennis Wheatley was reportedly also a factor). And so the band metalheads idolize, even today, was finally born.

They were still playing blues material, churning out songs based around three chords. But they were also beginning to experiment and move outside of the box a little, "because it was so simple," Geezer explained. "Then you get bored of that so you go on to some other bits and you can feel yourself progressing all the time. Eventually you've got the background to go and write your own songs. We were up against bands that were just starting, like Ten Years After, Jethro Tull, and Zeppelin. We knew we had to be as good as them to make a go of it. We knew we had to practice every day and rehearse every day to get as good as them, or to be good at all!"

The new material wasn't getting them attention, though. So it was time to try other tactics to make an impact. At one show Ozzy painted his entire body purple, hoping it would shock the audience into listening. It didn't—and it took him weeks to get all the paint off. So instead of subtlety, the band decided to hammer the crowd into submission. They kept increasing the volume levels until people simply couldn't hear themselves talk, and were forced to listen to the music. So people listened—but the band was still broke.

"We were starving, literally starving," Ozzy said. "If it hadn't been for Tony's mum, I don't think we would have survived at all. She used to make up all the sandwiches and give us cigs."

Ozzy's musical inspiration had been the Beatles, and he got the chance to literally follow in their footsteps in 1969 as Black Sabbath was given the opportunity to play the Star Club in Hamburg, the exact place the Fab Four had spent months honing their music at the beginning of the sixties, before they went on to change the world.

It was grueling, with them playing seven forty-five-minute shows a night. But it helped them in a way no amount of gigs in Britain could have. It made them tighter as a unit and bonded them as people—four foreigners in Germany, where they didn't speak a word of the language. And they were successful there in a way they'd never imagined, breaking the crowd record for the club that had been set by . . . the Beatles.

Could that have been an omen? They all hoped so.

With a name like Black Sabbath, it was perhaps inevitable that they'd find themselves associated with black magic. However, they hadn't expected to be asked by a group of Satanists to play a gig— and at the ancient symbolic site of Stonehenge.

More than a little nervous, they refused, only to be told that a curse had been placed on them. The band's reaction was simple— Ozzy got his machinist father to make some aluminum crosses, which they began wearing constantly for protection.

Aside from that scare, things finally began to move ahead for them after their time in Germany. They went down to Regent Sound studio in London and cut some more demo tracks, including "Evil Woman" and "The Rebel." That, in its turn, led to their first proper album, recorded and mixed in two days. It was just their live set, reproduced in the studio, and, according to Geezer, "the only difference with us is Tony did an eighteen-minute guitar solo on 'The Warning' and that was cut down by the producer for the album *Black Sabbath*. We didn't have any control whatsoever over that. We weren't allowed in on the mix."

But even though they'd been captured on tape, that didn't automatically mean an album would appear. Jim Simpson was turned down by fourteen record companies before he could find one that would take a chance on the band. Finally, on February 13, 1970, Vertigo Records released *Black Sabbath*.

"Musically, they are completely uncompromising, and would rather starve than sell out to more commercial forms of music," read the label's press release. But underneath, they were all hoping it would sell in huge quantities.

For Ozzy, it was a major moment in his life. He had a piece of vinyl he could take home and play for his parents. He'd made something of himself in rock'n'roll.

"I didn't even think about making a record when we made the first album," he recalled. "I was just pleased to be able to say: 'Look Mum, look what I've made—my voice on a piece of plastic forever.' "

But it was hardly the singalong radio music John and Lillian Osbourne preferred. When the needle clicked off after the record ended, there was a moment of unsure silence before John turned to his son and asked, "Are you sure you're only smoking cigarettes?"

HOW TO BE AN OZZY PARENT:

Show how happy you are when your kids achieve their goals.

The album climbed to number eight on the U.K. album charts and later that year reached number twenty-three in the U.S., where it was helped by a tour that began with dates in New York, working across the country to California.

By then, however, Sabbath had seen their popularity soar in England, playing dates around the country (and breaking the house record at Simpson's club) to ever-increasing crowds.

They were popular, and in the early seventies that meant one thing—it was time to go back into the studio. These days bands might take two or more years between albums. Back then they were expected to crank out two albums a year.

So in September they returned to the studio, to enjoy the extreme luxury of having four whole days to make their record. It was originally scheduled to be called *War Pigs,* after some of the tales about Vietnam they'd heard from American airmen stationed in England, but the record company wasn't too pleased by that idea. Instead, the album took its title from a track recorded right at the end of the session. Intended as nothing more than filler, "Paranoid" was knocked off hurriedly. Little did any of them imagine they'd just created heavy metal's first classic anthem.

Once out of the studio, they actually had more important things on their minds—more touring, and then they were going to America for the first time, to tour colleges. Now this was success, the way they envisioned it. Travel, luxury, see other continents. It was the big time.

It started out with a U.K. tour to mark the October 1970 release of *Paranoid,* an album which put them on top, quite literally, going all the way to number one, while the title track single managed number twelve. But with the big time and fame came complications they hadn't expected. At the Newcastle show, for example, a rowdy, drunken crowd, attracted by the band's chart success, invaded the stage during the first number and stayed there for the entire seventy minutes of the band's set. By the time it was all over, the P.A. had been destroyed, drum microphones had been stolen, and Sabbath was beginning to realize that this fame lark might not be all it was cracked up to be.

"If it means us having to give up putting out singles then we will," a stunned Ozzy said. "We want people to listen to us, not try to touch us. I was really terrified, shocked out of my mind."

But when an audience simply wanted to sit stonily and listen, they weren't happy, either. Playing in New York, the audience in the club just didn't want to know, and wouldn't get involved beyond sitting and paying attention—not until Bill Ward became frustrated and threw his drum kit at them. After that things livened up a bit, and they ended up playing seven encores.

There was no doubt they loved the freedom of America, especially the nubile groupies who were all over them. And the musicians, all young and single, didn't put up much resistance.

"When you're a kid . . . and you come from Aston to the States and you see all these f***ing c**ts wanting to be f***ed, you go like a bull at the gate."

Ozzy was single, but he did have a girlfriend at home, by the name of Thelma Mayfair, and when he returned from the States, at the beginning of 1971, they were married. She already had a five-year-old son, Elliot, from her previous marriage, and Ozzy adopted him. They'd go on to have two children of their own, Jessica

OZZY LOVES TATTOOS.

Ozzy might have complained when daughter Kelly got a tattoo, but she's really only following his example—he's a veritable walking gallery with seventeen of them . . .

1. *A flaming dragon head on his right chest*
2. *A Japanese fish head on his right middle arm*
3. *A heart and dagger on the lower inside left arm*
4. *Unidentified design, lower left arm*
5. *Dagger with OZZY, lower left arm*
6. *Full sleeve design, right arm*
7. *Stylized female vampire head and bat, upper left arm*
8. *Heart, upper left arm*
9. *Rose and SHARON, upper right arm*
10. *Unidentified letter, lower right arm*
11. *Shamanic figure, left thumb*
12. *MUM AND POP, lower right arm*
13. *Dagger, upper left leg*
14. *Cloaked death head, left chest*
15. *Smiley faces, both knees**
16. *OZZY, knuckes of left hand**
17. *THANKS, left palm**

Done in jail by Ozzy himself.

Starshine ("I wanted to call my daughter Burt Reynolds, but my wife wouldn't have it,") and Louis, affectionately nicknamed Bombins.

In the early 1980s, Ozzy would introduce his Elliot to marijuana.

"I said to him, 'Son, I'd prefer you to smoke this than tobacco.' He says, 'Why, Daddy?'

"I says, 'Because you can't physically smoke as many cigarettes of marijuana as you can of tobacco, because tobacco is the subtle drug of all. Because you don't realize. It's such a f***ing. You smoke a big fat joint and you're dead—you're crashed."

The marriage wasn't too successful. But it would have been hard to hold any relationship together. When Ozzy wasn't in the studio, he was on the road, all too often in another country.

HOW TO BE AN OZZY PARENT:

Try and spend as much time with your kids as possible, if you want to be close to them.

Black Sabbath had become huge, especially in the U.S., where "Paranoid" remained in the charts for an unbelievable sixty-five weeks. They were the exact opposite of the hippie peace-and-love idea that had been in fashion since 1967, and which had never really appealed to earthier middle America anyway. What they wanted was what Sabbath was offering—working-class music with plenty of underlying aggression. By virtue of its chart success, it was pop music, but it was also doing something different and new, finding places in people that most bands weren't even trying to reach. Only Led Zeppelin (two of whose members, Robert Plant and John Bonham, also came from Birmingham) were hitting a similar crowd.

"We've obviously got what the people want," Ozzy said at the time. "It's aggressive music and I think America likes aggression."

So when they were touring the U.S.—which they seemed to be doing constantly during 1971 and 1972—the crowds were responding. Whatever Sabbath wanted, Sabbath got—and they were eager to lap it all up: the free drink, the drugs, and the girls.

"When I first came to the States, I f***ed everything in sight," Ozzy recalled a few years later. "I've had the clap more times than f***ing God. I remember one occasion, we did Virginia Beach. The door knocks. I've just spoken to my wife . . . put the phone down and the door knocks. This beautiful chick comes in, and 'F***, I'm happening tonight!' I get her on the bed and I f*** the ass off her. She goes. Knock-knock-knock on the door. I think she's forgotten something . . . it's a different chick at the door. Beautiful as f***ing God! I swear she looked like an angel. And I f*** the ass off this one. She goes. Knock-knock-knock, and I'm thinking, 'I can't believe this.' Three—five chicks come in, and I f***ed five different—where are these chicks coming from? Where are these chicks coming from?"

HOW TO BE AN OZZY PARENT:

Tell your kids to use a condom if they have sex.

BANDS HEAVILY INFLUENCED BY *BLACK SABBATH*

1. Metallica

2. Marilyn Manson

3. Soundgarden

4. Iron Maiden

5. Pantera

6. White Zombie

7. Ministry

8. Megadeth

9. Widespread Panic

10. Faith No More

11. Henry Rollins

DID YOU KNOW THAT...

Ozzy can play the harmonica? He's featured on the instrument on "The Wizard" from *Black Sabbath*.

Ozzy featured his son Louis on the cover of his album *Diary of a Madman?*

On their first U.S. tour, Sabbath performed at the Whiskey in L.A. wearing white ties, top hats, and tails, and carrying canes?

Ozzy won a Grammy? It was Best Metal Performance for "I Don't Want to Change the World" from the album *Live and Loud* in 1994.

Ozzy once sang with Miss Piggy? Their duet, of the Steppenwolf classic, "Born To Be Wild," appeared in 1994 on *Kermit Unplugged*.

Ozzy collects Victorian art?

Ozzy and Sharon also own a farm in England, a hundred-acre retreat in Buckinghamshire?

One of Ozzy's former homes in L.A. was once owned by actor Don Johnson and his wife, Melanie Griffith?

Ozzy once shaved his head in the early eighties? It was because of problems caused by hair products.

They were stars, and they were getting the royal treatment. Everywhere they went in America, all doors were open to them, and they were happy to walk through. Very quickly they developed a reputation for wild living on the road, which suited them just fine.

But for all the albums they'd sold, and the chart success of "Paranoid," there was very little money flowing into their bank accounts. Throughout the 1960s, bands had gone through management problems—that was hardly anything new. Now Sabbath was going to begin to understand all the horror stories they'd heard in the past. And this was real-life horror, not black magic. It was business—the nightmare of every musician—and it was just beginning.

The Ozzman Goeth—
and Comes Back
with a Dove

Jim Simpson had done a good job for Sabbath. He'd taken them from nothing and helped them become stars, the real rock stars they'd always wanted to be.

Rock stars make money, a lot of money. And there's always someone hungry to take part of it. Which is what happened in Sabbath's case. With "Paranoid" high on the charts, the band was wined and dined—literally—by two guys, Patrick Meehan and Wilf Pine, who'd recently set up in business on their own after working for a manager with a dubious reputation, Don Arden, who'd been in the business almost since rock'n'roll began in Britain.

The band was picked up in a chauffeured limousine, and taken for dinner with all the champagne trappings at the Speakeasy, *the* club where the rock stars hung out in London. Meehan and Pine insisted that Jim Simpson had been mismanaging them, and that they would see a lot more money with the team of Meehan and Pine.

The words were falling on fertile ground. The band did believe they were making less money than they should, and weren't happy that Simpson was honoring bookings made months earlier, which had been set at a much lower rate than they were earning now. And so they signed with the young team, which would end up meaning years of litigation between Sabbath and Simpson.

But it didn't exactly bring happiness or riches to the boys. Sharon Osbourne would later claim that Black Sabbath made "nothing, I mean nothing," during the first part of their career.

HOW TO BE AN OZZY PARENT:

Remind your children not to believe everything they're told by strangers.

However, it felt as if they had all the trappings of success. If they wanted a new car, they asked their managers, and it was delivered (although Ozzy managed to wreck his Jaguar the day before he was due to sell it). A new house? No problem. They assumed they owned all this stuff, that it was all coming out of the money they'd earned. According to Ozzy, they learned that wasn't true when they parted ways from Meehan and Pine in 1974. In fact, most or all of it belonged to the management company.

Before that time, however, Sabbath was constantly busy. September 1971 brought the *Master of Reality* album, which included the ode to marijuana, "Sweet Leaf," and landed at number five in the U.K. charts and number eight in the U.S., where they spent a large amount of their time, bringing in a wide audience, as Geezer noted in 1972: "People keep calling us a teenybop band, thinking that we only appeal to people below the age of twenty. It's not true, we get a lot of heads at our concerts these days."

The drink, drugs, and groupies situation escalated on their tours, as the rumors spread that the band enjoyed a wild time, and there were always plenty of people ready to see they had one. In true rock star fashion, hotel rooms were trashed, there were plenty of stories about Ozzy urinating out of hotel room windows. The reputation for black magic and Satanism that had dogged them since their first album continued, and certainly songs like "Hand of Doom" and "Children of the Grave" hadn't done anything to lessen it.

It led to some strange scenes. On tour in Memphis, Tennessee, they found their dressing rooms decorated with crosses painted in blood, while a Satanist carrying a sacrificial knife jumped onstage during the show. Later that night, a witches' coven gathered outside the hotel, forcing Tony Iommi to invent a fake hex to get rid of them.

There were also threats that the band would be shot as they played. So when during a concert the lights failed after the third number, plunging the theater into darkness, Ozzy remained frozen, petrified with fear, at the microphone.

But they survived, and went back into the studio to record the adventurously titled *Black Sabbath Vol. 4*. Reportedly, the album's original title was *Snowblind*, a reference to cocaine, but their record company said no. Tales of the recording sessions have the band spending a lot of time in Jacuzzis, using cocaine.

HOW TO BE AN OZZY PARENT:

Tell your kids not to use drugs. In the end, no good can ever come of it.

Ozzy had become a father for the first time when Jessica was born (Louis would follow in 1975), and he and Thelma were living in the country—at least, when he wasn't on the road with the band. And it was a true country life; they even kept chickens, which led to an unfortunate Ozzy incident. One day, Thelma insisted it was Ozzy's turn to feed them. Needing nothing more than absolute peace, a frustrated Oz did go to the chicken coop. But instead of food he was carrying a shotgun and killed all of them—an act which didn't do anything to help tame his wild image.

Following the success of *Black Sabbath Vol. 4,* which hit number eight in Britain and number thirteen in America, they tried to widen the musical parameters a little on *Sabbath Bloody Sabbath.* It also marked their first attempt at recording somewhere that wasn't a studio, instead renting an English castle. And it was here that they began to wonder if dark forces might really be working against them. On the very first night Ozzy fell asleep in a chair in the main hall as a fire burned in the grate. Mysteriously, a piece of coal fell from the fire, and the room began to go up in flames. Ozzy escaped just in time, and the fire was put out. Then the band saw a figure walk into one of the rooms. Not knowing who it was, they decided to follow him inside . . . but there was no one there, and the only other exit was locked.

Singing about spookiness was one thing; living it was another. They packed their bags and left. But *Sabbath Bloody Sabbath* was eventually finished, with help on keyboards from former Yes man Rick Wakeman, bringing more depth to their sound. The album also marked Ozzy's songwriting debut, coming up with both lyrics and music for "Who Are You?" Mostly, however, they wrote in the way they always had: "Tony would come out with a riff, then I would put the bass in and Bill Ward would drum along," said Geezer. "Ozzy would instantly put a lyric or a vocal melody on top. You actually would hear the song the way it was going to end up. You knew immediately if it's going to work or not and where to put the bits in what songs. The collaboration was immediate and it was all there."

The success of the disc showed they hadn't lost any fans—it climbed to number four in the U.K. and number eleven in the U.S. on its release in early 1974. While making it, and for a while after, the band took a much-needed break from live dates, and had nothing planned until later in the year. They were therefore astonished when Meehan and Pine told them they *had* to play Cal Jam in Ontario, California on April 6. They hadn't rehearsed—and the news only came on April 5. There were going to be 450,000 people there, and the band simply didn't want to play the show without any chance to rehearse. But when they protested, their management threatened them with a lawsuit. So they trooped onto a plane and played in California, each receiving a thousand-dollar paycheck for the gig. They were unhappy with the show, but the money seemed fair. Or it did until they learned that the fee for Black Sabbath's appearance had been $250,000.

Meehan and Pine were fired. And all the cars and trappings of wealth suddenly vanished.

Sabbath decided it was time to try managing themselves. At least they weren't about to rip themselves off. But they had no management experience, and precious few business skills. It wasn't a good time. After taking more time off, they arranged a U.S. tour in three legs with a break between each to quell the exhaustion they'd experienced before. While the others reportedly remained fond of drugs, Ozzy became more and more attracted to alcohol, leading to the memorable interchange:

Reporter: Do you have a drinking problem?
Ozzy: Yes, I can't find a bar.

He was drinking to excess, and slowly becoming estranged from the band, even as they experienced their biggest success yet, playing New York's massive Madison Square Garden for the first time.

They did get back into the studio to make *Sabotage*, released in 1975, whose song, "The Writ," allowed them to vent their feelings about previous management problems. But they'd always gone with the flow they felt.

"We never were afraid to do whatever we felt at the time," Geezer said. "I think that's what kept us as Black Sabbath. Listen to anything past the first three albums; we do soul stuff, not what everybody else would do, but there's funky bass lines in there or funky guitar in bits, some synthesizers ('Who Are You') and straight-ahead ballads ('Changes'). Anything. We thought it would kill the band if we weren't allowed to grow up within it."

Making number seven in the U.K. and number twenty-eight in America, it kept them in the public eye. But they knew that to carry on properly, they needed a new manager. And in Don Arden—the former employer of Meehan and Pine—they thought they'd found the sharpest.

Arden had been around the business for a long time. Among others, he'd managed rocker Gene Vincent, the Small Faces, and was handling the affairs of Sabbath's fellow Brummies, ELO. He had a tough reputation, not to be taken lightly, and he didn't like being crossed.

Working in his office as a receptionist was his daughter, Sharon, then just eighteen. When Ozzy arrived for a meeting with Don, wearing a faucet on a chain as a necklace, and sitting on the floor after refusing a chair, the young girl was terrified of him, getting one of the others to bring him a cup of tea so she wouldn't have to face him herself. It was an inauspicious start to what would prove to be one of rock's most enduring, and interesting, marriages.

Arden quickly sorted out the band's business affairs. He lined them up with NEMS Records in Britain, with all their back catalog available again (in America they'd remained with Warner Bros.), and they celebrated with a U.K. tour, followed by another wild trek across America as the double album compiling their best material so far, *We Sold Our Souls for Rock'n'Roll* was released. While it didn't do as well as previous releases, only reaching number thirty-five in the U.K. and number forty-eight in the U.S., at least it kept their name on fans' lips, and the chart showing meant that Sabbath hadn't fallen out of favor.

For their next disc, they tried to experiment even more. *Technical Ecstasy* saw more gentle songs, and the vocal debut of drummer Bill Ward. While it satisfied the creative urges of three-quarters of the band, it didn't make Ozzy happy. For him, the way it used to be—hard, heavy, and direct—was the way to go. To him, *Technical Ecstasy* was a long way from headbanging heaven.

He'd been trying to cope with his personal problems, the excesses of alcohol and drugs. He'd even begun seeing a psychiatrist, although, he noted, their meetings weren't always too productive. "He plays mind games. He asks things like 'Do you masturbate?' and I say 'Do you breathe?' "

The craziness was out of hand, especially when they were on tour. Ozzy claimed that he and Bill took LSD every day for two years.

"I'm a guy that can't take a f***ing pill—I've got to take fifteen. I've got to go everything to the f***ing end. I can't have a drink, I've got to get bombed. I've got to take everything to the end. Everything. Life!"

He was going one way, and the band was going another. The result was that *Technical Ecstasy* was a dissatisfying album for everyone. Tony Iommi had even wanted to bring in a horn section, much to Ozzy's fury. On its release, the best it could manage was number thirteen in Britain, and only a disheartening number fifty-one in America. Ozzy was certainly dismissive of it: "What happened to *Technical Ecstasy* sales wise? I think it entered the Mongolian chart at three hundred and one."

Something had to crack, but the catalyst wasn't what anyone expected or wanted. On January 20, 1978 John Osbourne died, just two years after retiring from his job. Already unhappy and suffering from his substance abuse, it threw Ozzy into a tailspin. On the surface he might not have seemed close to his parents, but he'd idolized his father, and having watched him die of cancer of the esophagus put him over the edge.

"What freaked me out more than anything else was the funeral. I was singing f***ing Paranoid in the church . . . Seconal, drunk . . . it blew me away."

HOW TO BE AN OZZY PARENT:

Don't be afraid to love. And don't wait to tell your family you love them.

Ozzy's initial reaction was to run away from everything. He told the band he was quitting, and talked briefly to another singer, Glen Hughes, about the two of them starting a band. Sabbath, meanwhile, replaced Ozzy with Dave Walker, who performed a few dates with them, and became involved in the writing of the next album.

Ozzy had a problem, and he knew it. He'd been told his liver was in danger if he continued to drink the way he had been. But after grieving for a while, he knew he couldn't do anything else. He needed to get back to music. And the music he knew was Black Sabbath. He wanted to come back.

Cautiously, the others agreed; after all, the success of the band had been the four of them together. They'd written an album's worth of material with Walker, but trashed it when Ozzy said he wasn't going to sing it. Instead they headed off to a studio in Toronto, Canada, to begin work on *Never Say Die*. According to Ozzy, the studio was only picked because the Rolling Stones had mixed an album there, and the band needed to spend time away from England for tax reasons. But they'd only written two complete songs before hitting the studio, and in the end, he claimed, the total cost of making the record was $500,000, for what he viewed as "the biggest pile of horseshit that I've ever made in my life. I'm embarrassed with that album."

HOW TO BE AN OZZY PARENT:

Don't be afraid to admit you're wrong.

Obviously, things couldn't continue. Ozzy's comeback had been short-lived and unhappy. While *Never Say Die* still claimed a place (number twelve) in the upper reaches of the British charts, it could only manage number sixty-nine in the U.S. It was over. In January 1979 Ozzy Osbourne was fired from Black Sabbath.

Actually, he'd wanted to simply quit. But on his lawyer's advice, he let himself be fired, since there was the possibility of claiming money from the band—which in the end didn't happen, because he said, they were "penniless."

At that point, according to Ozzy, Sharon Arden was the effective manager of Sabbath. Ozzy knew he was going to continue in music, but with no idea who his manager might be—Don Arden and his daughter, after all, managed the band. For three months he lived in Los Angeles, living in a cheap hotel and drinking heavily, trying to figure out his next move.

It was Sharon Arden who saved him—the first of many times in the years to come. She and her father had decided that the future lay with Ozzy, not Sabbath, and they not only wanted to manage him, they also wanted to sign him to Arden's label, Jet.

The time had come for him to put a new band together and start the rest of his life. Coming on board were some veteran rockers, Lee Kerslake, who'd drummed with Uriah Heep, and Bob Daisley, who'd been the bassist in Rainbow, the outfit formed by ex-Deep Purple guitar hero, Ritchie Blackmore. The linchpin, however, would be the guitar player—one of the most vital components in a metal band.

Enter Randy Rhoads. Just twenty-three, he'd been a member of Quiet Riot, and had already recorded a pair of albums with them. A native Californian, he'd been inspired by Sabbath and bands like them, and was one of the hotshot young guitar players on the scene—but was largely unknown.

Ozzy had auditioned hundreds of players through what he admitted was a drunken haze. None of them measured up to what he needed, someone stunning and completely original, but also able to rock like crazy.

Randy was introduced to Ozzy through musician Dana Strum, and arrived for his audition at the appointed time. It was a major moment in his life—after all, Ozzy was one of metal's founding fathers and one of the music's great heroes. To his astonishment, he'd barely plugged in and tuned up when Ozzy told him that he had the gig.

Suddenly, instead of simply being one quarter of a band, Ozzy was plunged into the position of being leader, with all the responsibilities that followed. Long estranged from his wife Thelma, and having filed for divorce, which would become final in 1981, he'd also started to become romantically involved with Sharon, who handled the day-to-day management of Ozzy for her father.

The band assembled, they headed to England to write and record their first album together. This was another defining moment for Ozzy. In Sabbath he'd mostly sung the songs given to him. Now he had to help deliver the goods himself.

Blizzard of Ozz, as both the band, and their debut album, would be called, quickly jelled, and the songs, mostly cowritten by Ozzy and Randy, came thick and fast. In the early summer they went into the studio and laid down the tracks, prior to playing their first gigs in the U.K.

Those first gigs, in fact, weren't under the band's real name, but as Law. They played a pair of low-key warm-up shows in Scotland, and wanted to keep the identity secret. They played the entire *Blizzard of Ozz* album and some Sabbath covers to rapturous applause. At that point Ozzy began crying.

For weeks he'd been terrified that he couldn't make it alone, that being a part of Sabbath—whom Arden had now dropped— was all he could do. And now he'd shown there was more depth to him than that. He not only could make it on his own, he could even be successful.

Under their real name, the band went on to fulfill their U.K. tour, including a show at the Reading Festival, prior to the album's appearance.

Appearing on Arden's Jet label, *Blizzard of Ozz* performed better than anyone could have expected, climbing to a surprising number seven on the British charts, although the single, future metal classic "Crazy Train," only reached number forty-nine. It was an affirmation that Ozzy could really be a star on his own, that he didn't need the Sabbath guys—in fact, for the best part of the next two decades, they'd rarely have a good word to say about each other.

One thing Ozzy didn't have, however, was an American label. His destructive, and self-destructive, behavior, had been well documented, and U.S. labels weren't even sure they wanted to take a chance on such a wild card, particularly one who hadn't proved himself yet as a solo artist.

Sharon Arden had to work hard on behalf of her new boyfriend. Eventually, given the U.K. chart-placing of the album, she was able to convince CBS that it was worthwhile to sign Ozzy. But the best she could manage was a paltry $65,000 fee, and that only covered one album—which was almost an insult given how many records he'd sold with Sabbath.

Truthfully, CBS really wasn't that interested in Ozzy. They'd signed Adam Ant, the new wave artist who'd been racking up hit after hit in Britain, and believed the Double O's time had come and gone, and that they might make back their money on him and a little profit, but without any great expectations.

Introducing him to his U.S. record company was Sharon's idea. By now she'd been around Ozzy enough to have adopted some of his wildness, although she could still be completely businesslike when necessary. The disagreements between them were legendary, arguments where Sharon would throw things, like bottles of expensive perfume, at Ozzy, who seemed to be out of it much of the time.

By all accounts, he was that way when he and Sharon were escorted into the boardroom of the CBS office in Los Angeles early in 1981, as part of the company's convention.

Sharon was carrying a case holding three doves. Her idea was to make a big bang by releasing the doves as he walked in. That wasn't quite what happened. Ozzy was drunk, lurched into the room, and sat in a girl's lap.

"I just thought, 'F*** it, I'll give this lot something to think about,' " Ozzy recounted.

And that was exactly what he did. According to Ozzy, two of the three birds were released. The third had died, and that was the one he picked up and bit the head off of as the CBS employees watched.

"I'm ninety-nine-point-nine percent sure it was alive," said one woman who worked for the company. "I remember I was leaning forward and thinking 'How cute,' and suddenly he bites its head off. . . . I think he ate the head; he started spitting some feathers out."

One woman began screaming. All the staff in the room had turned white with shock. No one had expected anything like this. Sharon, by her own admission, began laughing so hard that she peed her pants, and "It wasn't just a little bit, it was a puddle."

The record company was outraged. Even by rock's standards, this was over the top—even more so as rumor has it that on the way out, Ozzy casually bit the head off of a second dove and threw it into the lap of a receptionist. There were threats to tear up the contract.

Inevitably, the story hit the press, and suddenly Ozzy was being called a "madman" and "insane," not that it worried him. "I don't mind being looked on as crazy," he said. "I mean, I make a good living at it."

Was it all a publicity stunt to put Ozzy back in the public eye? Although it's been denied, the possibility exists. Or was Ozzy simply determined to shock a bunch of jaded record executives, to be as outrageous as possible? Or was he simply completely out of it, and not fully aware of what he was doing?

More than two decades later, does it even matter?

What he did was create one of the defining moments of the Ozzy legend. Rockers had outraged before, but no one had ever gone this far. To actually bite the head off a dove . . . it took everything to a new level.

HOW TO BE AN OZZY PARENT:

Tell your kids being trashed is never an excuse. Tell them not to get trashed in the first place.

Columnists raged against Ozzy. CBS banned him from their office building. The Humane Society of America tried unsuccessfully to get his upcoming tour halted.

OZZY'S DISCS FOR A DESERT ISLAND

Sgt. Pepper's Lonely Hearts Club Band, *The Beatles*

Revolver, *The Beatles*

Rubber Soul, *The Beatles*

The Beatles *(AKA* The White Album*)*, *The Beatles*

Led Zeppelin I, *Led Zeppelin*

Led Zeppelin II, *Led Zeppelin*

Band on the Run, *Paul McCartney and Wings*

Arc of a Diver, *Steve Winwood*

Hello, I Must Be Going, *Phil Collins*

Kissing to Be Clever, *Culture Club*

Essence to Essence, *Donovan*

Notably, however, the label put out *Blizzard of Ozz* while the incident was still fresh in peoples' minds. It immediately rose to number twenty-one—and has since gone quadruple platinum. It wasn't just people into metal who knew Ozzy's name now, it was everyone in America, thanks to the coverage the dove incident had received. He'd become, quite literally, a household name overnight.

The band that toured the U.S. in 1981, however, was not the same one that had made the album. Gone were Kerslake and Daisley, replaced by Tommy Aldridge (who'd been in the band fronted by guitarist Gary Moore, who'd also been managed by Sharon Arden) and bassist Rudy Sarzo, who'd been in Quiet Riot with Rhoads.

If it seemed he'd been as outrageous as he could get, the fact was he'd barely begun. At the end of each show, he took to catapulting raw meat—usually things like stomachs and intestines, in a weird throwback to his slaughterhouse days—into the audience. The crowd was more than happy to respond in kind, bringing their own meat to throw at Ozzy. He knew it had gotten seriously out of hand when "we had to turn this guy away from our show because he was trying to get in with an ox's head, a full head!"

The dove incident and its aftermath brought them publicity, but it backfired in a way. It removed the focus from the music, and people expected Ozzy to be more and more outrageous every night. He could be as crazy as the best of them, but not every single time.

"We got attention as a result," Sharon remembered, "but the stuff about sawing the legs off a Doberman and blowing up small animals was pure fabrication."

However, the American tour had two positive results. It transformed Randy Rhoads from just another lead guitarist into one of the great axe heroes, and it brought Ozzy and Sharon closer than ever, although their relationship continued to be tempestuous.

"Our fights were legendary," she recalled. "We'd beat the shit out of each other. At a gig, Ozzy would run offstage during a guitar solo to fight with me, then run back on to finish the song!"

His divorce from Thelma had become final, and Sharon and Ozzy became engaged. While she was managing Ozzy, his contract was with her father, Don. Since she was so involved with Oz on every level, it made perfect sense to her that she become his official, contracted manager. But when she asked Don if he'd sign Ozzy over to her, the man refused—it wasn't good business. She could buy him out—for $1.5 million.

That was easier said than done. Ozzy might have been a word on everyone's lips, but as a solo artist he hadn't become a major property yet. The album had yet to go platinum. But somehow she managed to scrape together the money, and paid her father what he demanded. However, it caused a rift between them that has never been healed. Don Arden has never met any of his grandchildren, and, as long as Sharon has a say in the matter, he never will.

HOW TO BE AN OZZY PARENT:

Stay on good terms with your kids. Someday they'll have kids of their own, and you'll want to see your grandchildren.

To capitalize on the popularity of *Blizzard of Ozz,* no sooner had the band finished touring than they rushed back to the studio to make another album, the ironically titled *Diary of a Madman* (although the name actually comes from the autobiography of occultist Alisteir Crowley). It was here that Rhoads truly shone, showing those who hadn't seen him in concert what he could do on guitar, and firmly cementing his god-like reputation as a player. Once again, the album went platinum in America, climbing to number sixteen (number fourteen in the U.K.), and showing that, far from being over the hill, Ozzy was just reaching the peak of his powers.

Once more, though, the lineup changed, with Daisley coming back on board to replace Sarzo, and another former Rainbow musician, keyboardist Don Airey, added to fill out the sound.

The dove had been the first pivotal incident in Ozzy's solo career, which continued its uninhibited wild streak. Neither he nor Sharon seemed to be very good at controlling themselves. They were rock's crazy couple, and they were reveling in it. Ozzy had proven himself. They were young, they could do what they liked, get away with anything, all seemingly with impunity.

Whatever Ozzy tried to do—the dove, the meat slinging—simply seemed to bring him more fans. And, of course, he produced some of the best metal music of the time, of any time, his partnership with Randy Rhoads being particularly fruitful. Rhoads certainly encouraged budding guitarists among the fans, often giving guitar clinics in towns where the band was playing, which made a lot of friends around the country. It looked as if the pairing would end up being one of rock's great ones, maybe even up

OZZY QUIZ

1. How many homes do Ozzy and Sharon own?

2. Where did they live before Beverly Hills?

3. How many times have the original Black Sabbath reunited?

4. How many movies has Ozzy acted in?

5. How many of Ozzy's albums have gone platinum in the U.S. (sold more than one million copies)?

6. How many solo albums has Ozzy released (not counting compilations)?

7. How much are Ozzy and Sharon worth?

8. When Black Sabbath performed at Live Aid, a benefit for those starving in Ethiopia, what song did Ozzy want to use to open their set?

9. What's Ozzy's recurring dream?

10. How many pairs of black sweat pants does Ozzy own?

OZZY QUIZ: ANSWERS

1. *Two—the Beverly Hills house, and a farm in England.*

2. *Malibu, right by the beach.*

3. *Twice. The first was for Live Aid in 1995, then again in 1998, for an Ozzfest show that culminated in a tour and live album.*

4. *Three. He played a priest in* Trick or Treat, *a band manager in* The Jerky Boys Movie, *and himself in* Howard Stern's Private Parts.

5. *All of them.*

6. *Twelve.*

7. *$58 million.*

8. *"Food Glorious Food" from the musical* Oliver.

9. *"I'm running down a corridor with doors, and every time I go past the doors, they open and people chase me. And whenever I'm in the dream—I can be chased by a herd of elephants—I always seem to end up back in the house where I was born in Birmingham."*

10. *Forty.*

there as the metal equivalent of Lennon/McCartney or Jagger/ Richards. After all, they'd already produced some classic tracks together, and they'd barely begun. The future was wide open. Well, as long as Ozzy didn't go completely crazy—which seemed to be a real possibility.

It's All
About the Bat

They'd barely begun the U.S. tour in January 1982 when it happened. The incident that would dominate Ozzy's career, and put the dove stunt in the shade.

For a while people had been throwing objects on the stage during Ozzy's shows. Rubber chickens, toys, anything—although Oz was a bit worried when someone threw a doll up there, thinking for a second that it was a real baby. There was plenty of meat, almost everything imaginable. But no one had ever thrown anything that was still alive at Ozzy before.

Given what went on at his shows, it was reasonable that Ozzy would believe the bat was made of rubber when it landed on the stage in Des Moines, Iowa, on January 20, 1982. Quite why he decided to bite it, though, was another matter. Maybe he was carried away by the performance. Maybe he was just egging the audience on. Twenty years later, no one, probably even Ozzy, remembers. And it doesn't really matter anymore.

The facts are simple. He picked up the bat, which had been

stunned by the lights, and believing it to be rubber, he bit into its head. That was when he discovered it was a real, living, breathing bat—and it wasn't happy about being bitten, and began flapping. According to some reports, it bit back. Whether it did or not, Ozzy wasn't happy. He was in a panic. Sharon, at the side of the stage, was also in a panic.

As soon as they'd finished, Sharon rushed Ozzy to the Emergency Room for a rabies shot. Those shots would continue for a week, a series which he described later as "one of the most horrible, painful experiences of my life."

He'd done it all by mistake, although, after the dove, no one really wanted to believe that. Even when he said, "if you want to be a complete d***, try it," no one wanted to believe him. After all, from a dove in a boardroom to a bat before a crowd was a very small step.

HOW TO BE AN OZZY PARENT:

Don't let your kids eat just anything.
Especially if it's not dead.

It made him into a marked man. The newspapers said, once again, that he was mad. He even called himself a "madman," admitting he could do nothing in moderation. But this was an entirely new level of craziness, and the defining moment of his career to many people, the one thing they'd remember. And it remains that way, twenty years later.

As he told it, "I've never eaten a bat. I thought it was one of those plastic ones and just put it in my mouth and spat it out." He'd rather forget it—but no one in the media will ever let him. "I get p***ed off with people asking me what bats taste of," he said in 2001. "F*** me, that was twenty years ago. I was watching some program called *Bad Asses of Rock'n'Roll* on VH1 recently and they had me at number one. I was like, 'How the f*** did they work that out?' "

Maybe it was a cumulative score. Ozzy could be wild, he'd certainly proved that, but he'd really barely begun, although he didn't know it yet.

The bat incident brought the dove incident back, and once again he was hounded by the Humane Society and the A.S.P.C.A., who not only protested his concerts, but also monitored them to ensure that no animals, small, large, or otherwise, were hurt while he was performing. One apocryphal tale had him throwing ten dogs into the audience, and refusing to appear until the dogs were returned to the stage—dead. It was an urban myth.

But then again, nothing seemed impossible when it had to do with Ozzy. He'd done so much, drunk enough alcohol and devoured enough drugs that almost any tale was accepted as true, no matter how far-fetched.

"It took a lot of water to down just that f***ing bat's head, let me tell you. It's still stuck in my f***ing throat, after all these years. People all over the world say, 'You're the guy who kills creatures? You still do it? You do it every night?' It happened f***ing once, for Christ's sake."

Still, a month later, on February 19, just as the bat fuss was beginning to die down, Ozzy had to go and do something that really could have gotten him killed.

As the saying goes, Don't mess with Texas. He not only messed with the state, but with one of its shrines—the Alamo. The tour had reached San Antonio, and by his own admission, Ozzy was extremely drunk in his hotel room, having consumed an entire bottle of Courvoisier brandy—enough to leave most people flat out, if not in the hospital with alcohol poisoning. To try and stop him from causing trouble, Sharon had stripped him and locked away his clothes, figuring that even Ozzy wouldn't leave the room naked.

She was right. Drunk as he was, Ozzy wasn't going to wander around without any clothes. But he did want to go and see the Alamo—the band's hotel was close by. Not finding anything of his own to wear, he put on one of Sharon's dresses. Not just any dress, but a ball gown. He picked up his camera, left the hotel, and began snapping pictures of the most famous historical monument in Texas.

HOW TO BE AN OZZY PARENT:

Tell your children that cross-dressing is okay in some circumstances.

Doubtless there were strange looks and comments as he wandered around, but Ozzy was oblivious to them all. He shot a whole roll of film while in drag, and was about to change rolls when the effects of the alcohol kicked in, and he needed a bathroom.

Of course, there wasn't one to be found. But there was an old wall which would do to pee against. And that's exactly what he began to do, enjoying the sweet relief.

What he hadn't realized was that the old, tumbling-down wall was a part of the Alamo.

That didn't go over well. A Limey rock star who'd recently bitten a bat, wearing a dress, drunk, and pissing on a Texas shrine. The miracle was that he was just arrested, rather than lynched. And dressed like that, there was no way that a San Antonio prison cell was fun, even for the few hours until Sharon could bail him out.

HOW TO BE AN OZZY PARENT:

Tell your kids to use the bathroom before they leave home, especially in Texas.

Ozzy was charged with defiling a national monument, and the mayor of San Antonio decreed he could never play in the city again (a decree which was actually lifted ten years later, much to the disgust of some citizens). To some Texans, he got off far too lightly.

"I can honestly say, all the bad things that ever happened to me were directly attributed to drugs and alcohol," Ozzy declared in a great understatement. "I mean, I would never urinate at the Alamo at nine o'clock in the morning dressed in a woman's evening dress sober."

It was simply one more event in an ongoing catalog of outrageous events. And none of them was particularly calculated—they were just the things that seemed to happen to Ozzy as he went through his life. He wasn't looking for trouble. It just walked up while he was drunk or wasted, tapped him on the shoulder, and said hello.

But so far no one had been hurt, besides Ozzy, and he really didn't care too much, or so it appeared. He wasn't so much living on the edge as not caring if he careened over from time to time, and everyone around him was just following in his wake.

It was a disaster waiting to happen. So far everyone had been lucky, as if something had been protecting them all from anything but minor mishaps. They were playing well, getting great responses around the country.

But things were beginning to change. Randy Rhoads had hinted he wanted to go back to college, to pursue a degree in classical guitar at UCLA, and that would mean leaving the band. It would make for an odd change, since he and Ozzy had become such a tight partnership, creating some wonderful songs, and sharing a stage presence that had become adulation. Already Randy had been hailed by fans and the press as one of the great metal guitarists. He'd developed fans around the globe, and his playing was a vital part of Ozzy's sound.

On March 19, they were both on the tour bus, traveling from Orlando, Florida, to Knoxville, Tennessee, for the next show. To break the journey, they stopped at a small airfield in Leesburg, Florida. The bus driver was also a licensed pilot, and while the band rested, he decided to rent one of the planes and go for a spin. Don Airey and tour manager Jake Duncan went up with him for an uneventful trip. After he landed, Rhoads and the band's seamstress, Rachael Youngblood, decided to go up, which surprised Ozzy, since both were petrified of flying. For some bizarre reason, the ex-wife of the driver/pilot had been traveling on the bus—doubly strange since the couple had just undergone an acrimonious divorce.

The pilot began making fake dive-bomb runs, buzzing the bus where the others were trying to sleep. What no one knew, and wouldn't until later, was that the pilot was flying on more than a wing—his system was heady with cocaine.

It'll never be known for sure, but it's generally thought that the pilot's last run coincided with his ex stepping off the bus. He saw her and decided to crash into her. Instead he misjudged. The wing hit the bus, causing extensive damage but no injuries. But it sent the plane out of control "and went through into a house, and it was just a f***ing nightmare," recalled Sharon. "The house caught on fire."

It wasn't just the house. There was someone in it, a deaf man who'd been unable to hear anything coming and get to safety. It was Ozzy who woke up and braved the flames to rush in, and he was the one who pulled out the deaf man. It was too late for the others, and they were pronounced dead at the scene.

"Had I been awake, I would have been on that plane, probably sitting on the f***ing wing," Ozzy said. It's a thought that's come back to him over and over since that day.

As Sharon said, it was a nightmare come to life. Rhoads and Youngblood were dead. The driver was dead. The band was in ruins. For a moment there were questions as to whether Ozzy could even carry on, especially in the hours after he'd acted as a pall bearer at Rhoads's funeral. But inside a week Sharon had him auditioning for a new guitarist, and planning to get back on the road.

As she explained it, he was "in a state of shock. I knew that unless we got up and did something, Ozzy would be over."

For some fans, the ones who'd idolized Rhoads, it was already over. There'd never be another one like him.

There had to be someone, though, and Ozzy selected Bernie Torme, who'd been a member of Gillan, and started making up tour dates. With the pressure of some very big shoes to fill, Torme only lasted three weeks, forcing another fast replacement, Brad Gillis of Night Ranger, who saw out the remainder of the tour.

Once it was done, everyone headed over to Hawaii for some well-deserved, and necessary, rest and relaxation. But there was something else planned. After a tempestuous up-and-down, on-again, off-again romance, Ozzy and Sharon were finally ready to tie the knot. They did so on the beach in Maui on July 4, 1982. Tommy Aldridge was Ozzy's best man, the bride wore white, and the groom was dressed up in a bow tie and formal white suit. Ozzy picked the date for the wedding because it would be easy to remember, being the same as Independence Day.

HOW TO BE AN OZZY HUSBAND:

Pick a date you'll never forget for your wedding. That way you'll never miss the anniversary, and your wife won't get mad at you.

At the reception, the band was playing traditional Hawaiian melodies, not exactly the kind of music generally associated with a heavy metal god. As the members of the band were there, it was a situation easily remedied. The band was kicked out, and their instruments given to the guys from Ozzy's band, who began serenading guests with selections from the Ozzy, Sabbath (including "Paranoid"), and Beatles songbooks, while the happy couple danced.

They could begin to put the past behind them, and move along. Ozzy wasn't any more sober than he had been, but now his manager and wife could at least look after him properly, and he trusted her completely. "When it comes to the merchandising and the financial side of Ozzy—the business decisions—I have complete and utter faith in my wife. Sometimes she's wrong, but most times she's right."

One thing that certainly hadn't vanished in the drunken, doped haze was his sense of mischief. He knew that Sabbath had recorded a live album of older material, with new singer Ronnie James Dio taking Ozzy's place. In fact, Ozzy had visited Geezer when he was mixing the disc in L.A., showing up unannounced on his doorstep one night, only to be picked up later by a cab driven by "as capable a loony as his fare was," according to Butler. It was, perhaps, coincidental that Sabbath had recently re-signed with Don Arden, the nemesis of Ozzy and Sharon.

But Ozzy had always been the voice of Sabbath, and he came up with an idea—to record his own live album of the old material, and get it out before the other one. That was fine, except for one thing: The members of his band, who were on hiatus, didn't even know most of the songs.

That, however, was a minor detail. Assembling Gillis, Aldridge, and bringing bassist Sarzo back into the fold temporarily, he booked two nights at The Ritz in New York, to record before an audience in the club.

There was very little rehearsal time.

"The band had to learn ten songs in five days, and record them (plus three others) the next night," noted Gillis. The second night was there as recording insurance. Was it sloppy? Of course. But the fans didn't seem to care. *Speak of the Devil,* which was known in the U.K. as *Talk of the Devil* crashed straight into the charts on its release, selling half a million copies in the first week to peak at number fourteen.

"Black Sabbath always had its cult audience," Ozzy said, his tongue a little in cheek, "like Pink Floyd in the old days. But it was never as big as this." He could even defend the disc with a relatively straight face, claiming, "it's a good quality album. It wasn't a thing to 'get at' Sabbath on. I just did it. I understand that Sabbath had an idea of putting a live album out themselves."

The digs extended further. On the cover, surrounding the lurid picture of Ozzy, was some writing, which could eventually be made out to read: "Howdy! Dial-A-Demon productions in conjunction with graveyard graphics proudly presents the madman of rock dumping into El Satanos toiletto." Within, though, there was a serious note, an inscription by Ozzy: "A tribute to Randy Rhoads, the axeman. That kid was my lifeline, you know? He was such a dynamic player and I'd rather not talk about it anymore because it cuts me up every day of my life. Randy Rhoads rest in peace and love."

In 1995 he'd make this assessment of Rhoads, whose influence obviously still lingered: "It wasn't so much that it affected my music, but I felt that I lost a very dear friend and a wonderful person. How do you explain it because if you hide something from someone how do you expect them to see it? He was the first guy to come along and give me a purpose because he would patiently sit there with me and try to work out songs with me. I will always remember him, and send him flowers every year on the anniversary. Life, you know, it's gone like a flash."

One of the conditions of Sharon becoming Ozzy's manager was that he clean up his act and get sober. Sharon herself had cut out her excesses, because, she realized, "We were in the gutter, morally, and I realized that if we both carried on, we'd wind up a washed-up pair of old drunks living in a hovel somewhere. So I stopped drinking."

The only way to get Ozzy into detox was to trick him. It certainly wasn't a place he'd go of his own free will. So when Sharon told him she was "going to teach him to drink like a gentleman," he assumed she was going to show him how the upper classes passed out—and he was willing to go along with that.

What he didn't know was that she'd booked him into the Betty Ford Center. Even after he was inside, he didn't understand at first, which only became apparent when he asked the attendants escorting him to his room where the bar was!

It was the first of several trips to rehab that Ozzy would take over the next few years, including more than one journey back to Betty Ford. But life on the road, with all the drink and drugs he could consume freely available to him, wasn't exactly conducive to a sober life. Perhaps the biggest hurdle was that Ozzy himself simply wasn't ready to be sober. He'd given up the groupies after becoming involved with Sharon—well, more or less; there had been an incident in Japan where Sharon flew in unannounced, and joined Ozzy in his hotel room, only to be awakened later when a groupie joined them. He was determined to make this marriage work, learning from his previous mistakes.

HOW TO BE AN OZZY HUSBAND:

You have to work at a marriage. It doesn't simply develop and last on its own.

"I was married to a woman before, but because of my alcohol and drug abuse, I screwed up the marriage and it affects the kids the most. They're the silent sufferers."

He did what he could for the kids he'd had with Thelma. "I feel a bit bad about not always being able to be there for them. But I have tried to compensate. I call them at least every week, and they're getting the best education money can buy." While he'd remain fairly close to both Elliot and Louis, he and Jessica would part ways, and stop speaking—her decision, not his.

Out of rehab, rested but not necessarily sober, Ozzy did something that shocked those who knew him—he shaved his head. For a metal star to do that in the early eighties was unheard of; rockers simply didn't get rid of their long hair then. It wasn't an act of any kind of defiance. It wasn't even something done by accident when drunk, the way he'd done so many things. Nor was it—as some speculated at the time—a result of the rabies shots. There was a reason behind it.

"I was using a lot of gels and oils in my hair, and with those bright stage lights beating down on that all night long, it was making my hair very brittle and damaged. So one day I just shaved it all off!"

And that was the way he looked when he appeared at the gigantic U.S. Festival in San Bernadino, California, bald-headed in front of a crowd of 350,000. A pregnant Sharon was being careful with herself, understandably. Still, that didn't mean she was happy with her husband's new "do." "I went home with my hair in a bag and my wife went insane," he laughed. "She bought me a Lady Godiva wig from a joke shop and I went onstage in it the next night."

But following the festival, Oz had a full schedule. There was another album to record, and a tour to undertake. It was, as he'd sung, a crazy train.

The personnel in the band seemed to be a revolving door. In came another new guitar player, Jake E. Lee, as Gillis returned to Night

Ranger, arriving just in time for the *Bark at the Moon* sessions. One of Ozzy's more popular records, eventually going double platinum— over two million copies sold—it rose to number nineteen in the U.S. and number twenty-four in England, showing that Ozzy remained as popular as ever, even though the fashions in music had come and gone since his time with Sabbath, and for the non-mainstream crowd, punk and other styles had become the order of the day.

"I didn't listen to it until it was over and then I was mad for it," he recalled. "It was the same kind of thing as we were getting across, but with all the stops pulled out. Sid Vicious was great. I met him once in the Rainbow Bar and Grill in L.A., but he was so stoned he didn't even know who he was."

Ozzy, however, knew just who he was, but in the video for "Bark at the Moon," he'd actually become someone else, just adding to his mythology by transforming into a werewolf on camera (which, to be fair, wasn't a change that surprised too many people). The shoot wasn't easy, requiring plenty of changes as filming pro-gressed, and a total of eight hours in makeup, enough to try the patience of many, although he accepted it well enough.

Bark at the Moon pushed at the boundaries of Ozzy's music in a way he'd never done before. Indeed, the band prepared more for this release than for any previous, actually recording demos of the songs before going into the studios. "So Tired" even introduced something people never expected to find on one of his records— the use of a full orchestra.

The song became another single, charting in Britain, and that meant another video, this time with Ozzy playing every role. It was also, literally, explosive, as the mirror used was shattered into pieces. It wasn't a special effect; the mirror used really did explode. Unfortunately, the charge used to detonate it was too strong, and shards of glass went into Ozzy's face and throat.

He insisted he was fine, but on the flight back to America after filming, ready to jump straight into a new tour, the cabin pressure caused serious problems. He was in agony, and the pilot ended up radioing ahead for an ambulance to meet the plane and take Ozzy to the hospital.

There were no permanent ill effects, and no seven years of bad luck, but he did have to postpone the first eight dates of the tour. And he also became a father again, as Sharon gave birth to Aimee Rachel Osbourne on September 2, 1983.

HOW TO BE AN OZZY PARENT:

Love your sons, treasure your daughters.

This was the era when heavy metal was out of favor with much of the public, the big exception being Ozzy. People just liked him. Filmmaker Rob Reiner made fun of the entire genre with his 1984 spoof documentary *This is Spinal Tap*, a film that laughed at the excesses of musicians—excesses that Ozzy knew only too well, as he lived them every day. "I thought it was a documentary about Black Sabbath!" he said. "I was the only person not laughing because I thought it was a serious program. I lived that life; it was just a real situation for me."

So how did Ozzy manage to stay in favor, and still sell millions of records when other metal acts could hardly get arrested? Simply by being Ozzy. He might terrify the general public, but to his fans, he was quite lovable. ". . . I've made a complete pr*** of myself so many times. But I got away with it, because I was Ozzy Osbourne and that gave me a license to be an a**hole."

He was the person his fans wanted to be, the wild man, the madman of rock, who bit the heads off doves and bats, who was a legend in his own lifetime. But who, now that he was a father again, since Sharon had given birth to another daughter, Kelly, on October 27, also readmitted himself to the Betty Ford Clinic in another attempt to kick the drugs and alcohol.

"I am something of a madman," he admitted. "I can do nothing in moderation. If it's booze, I drink the place dry. If it's drugs, I take everything and then scrape the carpet for little crumbs. I took LSD every day for years—I was spending about one thousand dollars a week on drugs . . . I OD'd about a dozen times."

He came out, but nothing had changed. There were still the drugs and the alcohol. But at least the animal welfare societies seemed to have forgiven him for his avian exploits. He'd donated $2,000—the money he'd received as part of the Ampex Golden Reel Awards for selling over a million copies each of *Blizzard of Ozz* and *Diary of a Madman*—to the A.S.P.C.A. In return, they'd given him a lifetime membership.

The rule seemed to be that wherever Ozzy went, trouble was certain to follow. It dogged him like a shadow, even when he tried to do a good deed.

Since quitting Black Sabbath, he'd barely spoken to any of the members, other than to trade insults in the press. But then came Live Aid. It had been organized by Bob Geldof (who's now Sir Bob Geldof because of it) to raise money for those starving in Ethiopia. Concerts would be staged concurrently in London and the U.S., and televised globally, with people calling in pledges.

It was one of the major musical events of modern times. Led Zeppelin, who'd disbanded in 1980 following the death of drummer John Bonham, re-formed for the event, with Phil Collins of Genesis behind the kit. If Zep could do it, why not Sabbath? It was for a good cause, and worth one day of everyone's time to help raise money.

Of course, it wouldn't have been Ozzy without some sense of mischief and mayhem. He was the one who wanted to start a benefit show for starving Ethiopians with "Food Glorious Food," from the musical *Oliver*—which didn't happen.

HOW TO BE AN OZZY PARENT:

Don't be afraid to volunteer your time and energy for a good cause.

Sabbath performed three songs to literally millions of people on television. They did their bit to alleviate hunger in the Horn of Africa. But it came at a cost. The day before they took the stage, Ozzy was served with a writ from Don Arden, alleging that he was trying to re-form Sabbath as a performing unit, and claiming $1.5

million in damages (coincidentally the same figure he'd charged Sharon to buy Ozzy's contract).

What was Arden trying to achieve? Was it part of the ongoing animosity between father and daughter, an attempt to hinder Ozzy's career? No one will ever know. But when it came to trial, Arden's suit was dismissed. It was quite apparent that neither Ozzy, Geezer, Tony, nor Bill had ever envisioned the show as being more than a one-time thing. There was a vindication in that, not just for the musicians, but for Sharon, too, who had no love for her estranged father.

Arden himself had been in the dock. He'd faced a trial in Britain on charges of false imprisonment and blackmail of business associates, but was acquitted (his son, David, was convicted on those charges and sentenced to prison).

With the small interruption of a reunion out of the way, Ozzy could return to his own career. That meant back into the studio to record *The Ultimate Sin,* eagerly awaited by his audience as it was his first album since 1983. Unfortunately, it wasn't one of his best efforts musically—"cheesy," as one fan described it. But the album that appeared, finally, wasn't the one he'd originally written. He'd composed a full record's worth of material, only to scrap it as not good enough, before going back into the studio to make this one.

Even then, things didn't go smoothly. There'd been yet another turnover of personnel, which complicated things, and *that* was before the furor with the cover. In its original version, it pictured three crosses atop a hill, and a girl quite obviously not wearing underwear. It didn't sit too well with the record company, and was replaced.

For what was often thought to be a weaker effort, it proved to be one of his biggest sellers, going to number eight in the U.K. and number six in the U.S., with "Shot in the Dark" becoming a hit single on both sides of the Atlantic. Ozzy celebrated the release by undertaking his first full British tour in three years, a full fifteen dates, which was pretty close to saturation level on a relatively small island, before returning, yet again, to the States to complete a tour before his third child with Sharon, a son called Jack, was born on November 8.

By the time he reached America, the fans, it seemed, were out of control. At the Meadowlands, in New Jersey, they caused $80,000 worth of damage to the stadium—which Ozzy covered out of his own pocket. But that would seem like nothing compared to what was to come.

HOW TO BE AN OZZY PARENT:

If your kids damage something, be prepared to pay for it yourself. After all, you're the one in charge. Then talk to them about it later.

Getting off a plane at LAX airport, Ozzy was besieged by reporters wanting to know what he thought of the lawsuit that had been filed against him. At that point he knew nothing about it—he didn't even know there was one. Finding out, however, was going to be a long process.

GUITARISTS WHO'VE PLAYED WITH OZZY

Tony Iommi

Randy Rhoads

Bernie Torme

Brad Gillis

Jake E. Lee

Zakk Wylde

Joe Holmes

Ozzy had been sued before, it was par for the course for a rock star. He'd been vilified by everyone from right-wing Christians to animal protection advocates. But no one had ever accused him of causing someone's death.

In 1984 a California teenager had shot himself in the head while listening to the song "Suicide Solution" from *Blizzard of Ozz*. In the wake of that tragedy, not one but three lawsuits had been filed

GEORGE W. BUSH IS REPORTEDLY A BIG FAN OF *THE OSBOURNES.* WHILE IT MIGHT NOT SEEM SO ON THE SURFACE, BUSH AND OZZY HAVE A LOT IN COMMON— AND A FEW THINGS TO SEPARATE THEM. . . .

1. George W. Bush is president of the United States. Ozzy is the president of Metal.

2. Both men are married to strong women, Laura Bush and Sharon Osbourne, respectively.

3. Both are parents. Ozzy has six children from two marriages; W. has twin girls, Jenna and Barbara.

4. Both men are multimillionaires.

5. Both W. and Ozzy have overcome serious drinking problems and are now sober.

6. Ozzy and George W. are both from large families. Ozzy was one of six children, Bush has five brothers and sisters.

7. Ozzy's children have never been arrested or convicted of anything. The Bush twins were both cited for underage drinking.

against Ozzy and CBS Records, claiming his lyrics caused teenagers to commit suicide.

The attorney hired by the dead boy's family claimed that on "Don't Blame Me," another of Ozzy's songs, there were tones known as "hemisyncs," which rendered the listener incapable of resisting what was being said in the song itself. He even hired an organization called the Institute for Bio-Acoustics Research, Inc. to listen to the song and give their findings. They said the hemisync tones (and hemisync tones really do exist; they're a patented process which utilize sound waves to increase the rate the brain assimilates and processes information) made the youth susceptible to the lyrics of "Suicide Solution." And since that wasn't quite enough, they said the song also contained subliminal lyrics, recorded one-and-a-half times the speed of normal speech, whose meaning would become apparent to the listener after several hearings. The lyrics in question supposedly contained the words "Why try, why try? Get the gun and try it! Shoot, shoot, shoot," followed by maniacal laughter.

A teenager committing suicide is a horrible thing, and never something a parent would want for a child, anyone's child. As Ozzy said, "I swear on my kid's life I never said 'Get the f***ing gun'!"

But there's another factor to be considered, even before thinking of legalities. It would take a very technical, and very twisted, mind to come up with a plan like that. And Ozzy just didn't—couldn't—think that way. He went in, recorded, went home, went on tour. He wasn't that technically minded, he wasn't inclined that way.

The California teen wasn't the only one to have committed suicide to the song. Two others had, and this lent some fuel to the arguments about hemisyncs and subliminal lyrics.

A religious organization called Truth About Rock also waded into the matter, putting out a leaflet that claimed rock music, in all its forms, was the source of depravity and suicide among teens, stating that "the Devil wants to destroy you and he is using rock music as a primary agent. But God has not given you life, only to have it choked out by the demented obsessions of rock musicians."

According to them, Ozzy once said: "Parents have called me and said, 'When my son died of a drug overdose, your record was on the turntable.' I can't help that. These people are freaking out anyway, and they need a vehicle for the freakouts."

If he did ever say something like that, the words have been taken far out of context. Music is a form of rebellion for teens, and has been since the days of Elvis in the 1950s. It's music your parents hate, and that sets each generation apart from the next. That's a positive. But when a kid is watching MTV (or any kind of TV) all day, as Truth About Rock claimed one suicide victim did, then it might be apparent to the parents that there's a problem (especially when, according to the leaflet, the kid in question said, "Dad, I just can't cope with the pressure!") that needs attention.

HOW TO BE AN OZZY PARENT:

Talk to your kids, find out about their problems. Be alert for depression and isolation. It's important.

The religious conservatives had always been against Ozzy, with his Satanic reputation and antics, but he was, in fact, a great dad himself, one who took time with his own kids. "The best time we had recently was when the whole family took a bath together," he said in 1986, and Aimee, then two-and-a-half years old, dunked him underwater. "When I'm with Aimee, I become two-and-a-half myself."

But what Ozzy did with his own kids, and however good his parenting skills, that carried no weight in a court of law. What his lawyer did was invoke the First Amendment, citing the freedom of speech that allowed Ozzy to write about any subject he chose. And there was an irony about it all, as the song had been intended as an elegy to the late AC/DC singer, Bon Scott, who had committed suicide.

The suit was thrown out of court, but that wasn't the end of things. Lawyers for the family appealed to the California Superior Court to have it reinstated, leaving it hanging over Ozzy's head for the entire year of 1986. It was only on December 19 that Judge John L. Cole refused the motion, stating that the case involved areas "clearly protected by the First Amendment."

Really, though, it was Ozzy who cut directly to the core of the matter, in the manner only he could. If he kept urging his fans to kill themselves, he pointed out, soon he wouldn't have any fans left—which wouldn't be a good career move. And while logic and Ozzy hadn't always gone together, in this case he was quite right.

The Truth
About Rock

Although he was spending a lot of time in court, Ozzy still did his usual amount of touring in 1986, bringing his personal brand of madness and mayhem to the U.S. once more, then on to Japan, while still finding time to be a part of the famous "Monsters of Rock" (and who better than he?) metal festival at Castle Donnington in England in August. But—and this was a rare move—he was forced to get rid of bass player Don Costa for being, according to Ozzy, "too crazy"—a definite first for the Ozzy camp. Ozzy claimed that Costa had a passion for slicing his knuckles on the cheese grater he'd strapped onto the back of his bass. And that made Ozzy look positively normal by comparison.

For several years, and now especially through the court case, Christian fundamentalists had equated Ozzy with the Devil, and he'd never complained that much. It had always seemed funny. But at the beginning of 1987, he had his revenge. He'd been offered a part in the metal movie *Trick or Treat,* and he took to it with relish—as it offered him the chance to be any fundamentalist's worst nightmare: Ozzy the Bible-thumping minister. Playing the part in complete Ozzy deadpan style, he was hilarious, with impeccable timing, and a delight in the small role that would prove to be his film debut.

However, there might have been a little divine retribution in the fact that a month after the film premiered in March, Ozzy got mugged. He was in New York, in the middle of Times Square sitting in the back of a cab—generally a pretty safe place to be—when someone stuck a knife through the window and demanded his money. Faced with a blade, even the man they called the Prince of Darkness wasn't going to argue. He handed it all over and the thief fled on foot.

Nineteen eighty-seven was shaping up to be yet another busy year for Ozzy. He was thirty-nine, but still incredibly popular with metal fans around the globe—in many ways his popularity simply increased as he grew older. First up came a concert video, *The Ultimate Ozzy,* which had been filmed in Kansas City the year before, a simple performance of his set. It still went gold, selling more than half a million copies.

But the more important work was ahead of him yet. Ozzy had never properly celebrated the partnership he'd enjoyed with Randy Rhoads, and Randy had been one of the cornerstones of his initial solo popularity, an excellent friend, one of the great players, and a strong writer. Ever since Randy's death, fans had been writing to his mother, asking if there was any more material, live or studio, that could be released.

She'd been in touch with Ozzy. He knew the demand was there from fans. It was mostly a case of finding the time to go through his archives, to discover what they held, and whether any of it made for good listening. In 1986, during the few weeks when he wasn't on the road or in court, he finally had the chance to do just that, coming up with plenty of concert tapes. He passed them to Max Spencer, the man who'd produced Ozzy's first three solo albums— the ones that had featured Randy and brought him fame. Taking the tapes into the studio, Spencer was able to pick out the best material and performances, and digitally clean up the sound.

While the tracks were songs that had all become Ozzy classics, the real hero was quite intentionally Randy, featured in his trade-mark solos with flying fingers. The album itself would be an Ozzy disc—in fact a double-disc—but by its very title, *Tribute,* it wasn't about the Oz man at all, but Randy.

And that was the way the fans took it, sending it to number six in the U.S. and number thirteen in Britain, eventually going dou-ble platinum. It wasn't an album Ozzy could tour, or that he even wanted to tour, although he would, of course, be going back on the road soon enough. By now he had yet another new guitar, twenty-one-year-old Zakk Wylde, who also led his own band, Pride and Glory, and Bob Daisley had returned to the fold once more on bass.

It had been a typically weird Ozzy series of events and coinci-dences that had led to Wylde joining up. He'd first heard that Ozzy was looking for a guitar player on, of all things, shock-jock Howard Stern's radio show. Ozzy was a frequent guest, as casually outra-geous as his host.

Wylde was desperate to audition for the position, but had no idea how to even begin tracking down Ozzy. But he could play; in fact, he made his living teaching the instrument in his home state of New Jersey. It wasn't until a friend, a music photographer, offered to pass on a tape, that Wylde even began to think he had a chance. The photographer was as good as his word, and Wylde's talent brought him first an audition, and then a position in Ozzy's band, his dream come true, landing right on the top of the heap at such a young age.

"I was playing in this s***hole with this little crap band that was going nowhere fast when this guy came up and asked me about auditioning for Ozzy. I thought he was on crack. It was worth a try. I put a tape together and some Polaroids and next thing I knew Sharon Osbourne had me on a plane to California. Being a Black Sabbath freak, I s*** myself when I plugged in and looked over to my right and there was Ozzy!"

At least he overcame his nerves quickly. Which was perhaps just as well for the rest of the band.

One thing Ozzy wasn't trying to do during 1987 was release an album of brand-new material. With *Tribute* selling so well, there was no pressure, and, like most other acts, he'd begun taking longer between albums.

He did, however, play one very important and unlikely date during the year—a gig at Wormwood Scrubs prison in West London, for the inmates. Still, it wouldn't have been Ozzy unless he'd included at least one tiny piece of mischief. In this case, with prison guards all around—and probably memories of the three times he'd been inside himself, on the other side of the bars—he managed to restrict his humor to the set list, covering one very famous, and very apt song, "Jailhouse Rock." Perhaps because of *where* it was performed, this is one Ozzy cover that's never appeared on any bootleg. Notably, he's never performed it since.

A year after that show Ozzy announced that he wanted to tour the world's insane asylums. To some, all that brought was a question: how would they ever let him out of the first one? Needless to say, it was a plan that made everyone laugh, but unsurprisingly, it never happened. And maybe, given the way he was, it was probably just as well. This was a man who never did anything by halves.

"There's not enough alcohol in the world for me," he said. "There's no such thing as moderation in Ozzy Osbourne's vocabulary. I've never had *a* pint in my life. It's all or nothing—whether it's drugs, sex, drink, falling in love, anything."

He'd lived that way a long time, and even his responsibilities as a family man didn't seem likely to make him quit. He'd been in and out of rehab more often than some people had had hot dinners, and it hadn't solved anything. Ozzy was simply Ozzy, and no one could make him change. If it was ever going to happen, it would probably have to come from within. As he'd note some years later in *Rolling Stone Online:* "The down side of being outrageous is that you have to go around explaining your f***ing self to people. If you're too cocky, somebody might just pull out a f***ing gun and cock it and blow your f***ing face off. You gotta be really careful what you bite off. Don't bite off more than you can chew. It's a dangerous world."

While he knew firsthand about biting off more than he could chew, he had, however, taken his marriage vows seriously. As he put it, "sex with groupies is meaningless. After ten years, I'd had enough."

But there was still the music to keep him somewhat focused. "As long as there are kids who are pissed off and have no real way in venting out that anger, heavy metal will live on." He was doing something he loved, making music his audiences lapped up, living a life that was essentially luxurious. He was a star. So it was no wonder he could say, "I suppose there's a lot of people that've got a better life than me. But I don't know, I feel very fortunate and very blessed."

And, of course, he certainly wasn't the man people thought he was. The public image was very different from the real Oz. "My private life is nothing like people imagine," he pointed out. "I'm not sitting here in a devil's mask and fangs and chewing on an old dead bat while I'm talking to you. . . . mention Ozzy Osbourne and people will be convinced I'm talking to you with my personal warlock in the room."

And sometimes the reputation that surrounded him left him frustrated. "When I die all the news reports will say, 'Ozzy Osbourne was found dead today. He was famous for biting heads off animals' . . . I've been in this business for the best part of twenty years. Do you think I'm proud of the fact that what I'm gonna be remembered for, when it comes to the art section of the history books, is as the man who bit the head off a dove, instead of a musician who did more touring than most and sold millions of records? I think to myself, Well it ain't much of a f***ing legacy to have, is it?"

But at least he'll be remembered, which is more than most people can claim. It proves that, in many ways, Ozzy has transcended music to become an entertainer, and possibly even more than that, a sheer force of nature.

"I can't stop him," Sharon said. "The only thing I can do is make sure he's not on the street and make sure he sleeps in a way that he won't choke to death on his own vomit."

That didn't seem likely any time soon; he was moving right along. With his new band, Ozzy returned to the studio to record his first album of fresh material since 1986's *The Ultimate Sin,* two years before. The very aptly titled *No Rest for the Wicked* would appear in October, going straight into the U.K. album charts at number twenty-three on the week of its release, and climbing to number thirteen in America. It was a sign that whatever he did— and with Ozzy it was definitely what he did, and not what he didn't do—his fans adored him, and there were still plenty of them out there.

But more than most acts, he went out to please his fans. He supported the album with a two-month U.S. tour, starting in Omaha and ending in Long Beach.

Ozzy had always worked hard for his popularity. He toured almost constantly, or so it seemed, and he made sure he gave his fans a show. On the brink of forty, he'd become the grand old man of heavy metal, and he'd never lost his edge, which was something those who paid good money to see him appreciated. You never knew what Ozzy might do, and that was half the fun. There was always going to be something, even if it was small, to outrage.

In this case, it had been the album cover—yet again. They were a constant problem for Ozzy. But then again, the original version of *No Rest for the Wicked* had shown him wearing a crown of thorns, and the three girls around him were holding crucifixes. Given the way the Christian right felt about him, the record company decided dis-

THE OZ MAN AND SHARON SPEAK:

"Of all the things I have lost, I miss my mind the most."—Ozzy

"With a name like Black Sabbath, we'd look a right bunch of idiots standing there with a flower in our hands."—Ozzy

"They're sweet, but they've got no balls. You want to take them home and give them a glass of milk. You wouldn't want to f*** them."—Sharon on the Backstreet Boys

"I didn't think anything we did was spectacular. I remember we thought, 'Let's just write some scary music.' "—Ozzy on Sabbath

"It's like a professional runner kicking the wall all day long."—Ozzy on smoking

"I've made many statements about being sober, and one I can really say is . . . sobriety f***ing sucks!"—Ozzy

"If you're a woman and you say no in business, they call you a b****. If you say yes, you get s*** on."—Sharon

"Well, this'll do for a job. I'll get stoned every day, f*** chicks, and not worry about waking up early in the morning for work. I loved it."—Ozzy on his Sabbath days

"We always used to get one toy each and something placed in our stockings, like a tangerine, some nuts, and an apple."—Ozzy on his childhood Christmases

"We go to movie stars' houses and we always feel like aliens. Ozzy drops his dinner on the floor. I follow him into the toilets to make sure he doesn't p*** everywhere, we just don't fit in with the beautiful people."—Sharon

"I'm sick and f***ing tired of that f***ing [Pearl Jam singer] Eddie Vedder. Get a job in f***ing McDonald's if you don't like it [fame]."—Ozzy

cretion was the better part of valor, and made a few small changes that would stop many of the cries of anger and blasphemy, although they wouldn't have been anything new to the Oz man.

One thing was definite, though. When he wasn't rabble-rousing out on the road, he was becoming a family man, happy simply to spend his time at home in the eighteenth-century farmhouse in Buckinghamshire, England, that he and Sharon had purchased (and which they still own; with its privacy, it's likely to be the location used if a second season of *The Osbournes* happens). He genuinely loved passing time with his kids, watching them grow, and playing with them. Like so many musicians, Ozzy was, at heart, just a big kid himself. The life he lived meant that he'd never had to completely grow up, and for him that was perfect; he never needed to.

There were very few he could look to in the business to see where his career should go from this point. The Stones were still doing it, releasing albums and touring, but they were different. In metal, everyone was younger than he. He was the trailblazer. He was the influence. Everyone cited him. And maybe it was just as well, since making a living from music was pretty much all he'd ever known, and it was all he could do. Ozzy was the court jester who was also the king.

And he was a king whose crown seemed secure for life. *Wicked Videos,* a collection of just three videos, went on sale in 1989 and was quickly proclaimed gold. A month later *No Rest for the Wicked* was certified platinum. Then, on June 4, Ozzy performed one of the first pay-per-view cable television concerts, a live airing of his date in Philadelphia, which he celebrated onstage by donating $15,000 to AIDS research (he made plenty of money, but he has always been generous to many causes, even though that's a side of him that's gone unsung. He even gave $1 to Oral Roberts when the televange-list was raising money so that God wouldn't take him home).

HOW TO BE AN OZZY PARENT:

Teach your kids to support good causes.

And he was back on the charts again, duetting with metal vixen Lita Ford on the ballad "Close My Eyes Forever," which clambered to number eight on the singles chart, his first singles success in three years.

Nineteen eighty-nine was the year the world changed again. The Berlin Wall came down, and Communism died a quick death. For the first time, Russia was an open country, and it put on a music festival, the Moscow Music Peace Festival. Exactly where the peace was in having a bill full of metal bands, however, was any-one's guess. With notorious names like Ozzy, Mötley Crüe, Bon Jovi, the Scorpions, Cinderella, along with Russia's Gorky Park, CCCP, and Brigada S, the Lenin Stadium was a mass of noise and madness. The Crüe were even more renowned for their wild behavior than Ozzy, but he was determined to outdo them. While they'd been known to snort cocaine, Ozzy went one better. Spying a line of ants on a popsicle stick, he rolled up a bill and snorted them without missing a single beat. It was one more incident for the ever-growing book of Ozzy legends.

But how far *could* he take it? He'd been living on the edge for the best part of two decades, and though he'd come very close he'd never yet toppled over. However it seemed to be just a matter of time before something very drastic happened.

That wasn't in his thoughts after returning home from Moscow. He simply wanted to relax and recharge around his family. And for a week, that's exactly what he did. Then he found a case of powerful Russian vodka he'd been given in Moscow, and which had made its way back with him. Downing four bottles—enough to give most people massive alcohol poisoning—he said to Sharon, "I've decided you've got to go," and began choking her.

Sharon managed to call the police, who hauled Ozzy off to jail. When he awoke the next morning he was facing a charge of attempted murder, to which all he could reply was, "You've got to be kidding, I don't remember a thing!"

It could have been the end of the road, not just for Ozzy's career, but also for his marriage; after all, not many unions survive strangulation. And it would have certainly meant prison time for Ozzy if Sharon hadn't decided to drop the charges.

"I didn't press charges but he went into rehab for three months. He was totally insane from all the drink and drugs he was doing, and well, these things happen."

HOW TO BE AN OZZY HUSBAND:

Never try to strangle your wife.

WHAT OTHER MUSICIANS SAY ABOUT OZZY AND SABBATH

Vinnie Paul (Pantera): The dude is a legend. I still remember the first time I heard the *Blizzard of Ozz* album. It sounded so fresh and it had almost the same impact as when I first heard Sabbath.

Dave Grohl (Foo Fighters): I love Ozzy . . . He was once considered 'The Most Evil Man in Rock' and yet he's the cutest and funniest guy in rock, too. He's just like a little kid . . . with a hash pipe in his mouth.

Bill Ward (Black Sabbath): He's certifiable. Well, actually, he is certified.

Lars Ulrich (Metallica): Without Black Sabbath there wouldn't be a Metallica.

It was a curiously philosophical way of looking at things, and maybe not what Ozzy really deserved, but they had a deep, deep bond that went beyond the fact that they were parents together. She loved him and he loved her, even though, way, way over the top on vodka, he'd tried to kill her.

Some stories have Ozzy quitting alcohol after coming out of rehab, shocked into sobriety by the fact that he'd tried to kill his wife. If that was true, then he did some serious backsliding, because Ozzy himself recalled that he'd been to a club in L.A.

called the Rainbow with former Small Faces/Humble Pie singer Steve Marriott and comedian Sam Kinison a couple of years later. "Steve Marriott went home that Friday and was dead on the Monday [he died in a fire at his English home on April 20, 1991], and Sam Kinison died shortly afterwards [actually in a car wreck almost a year later]. And that was the last time I took a drink."

However and whenever it happened, Ozzy was now sober. And that was, perhaps, the most important change of his entire life. It had taken many attempts—a total of fourteen times in rehab, according to some counts—but he'd finally managed to overcome his problem. Well, perhaps not overcome it, but at least put it at bay. As he understood, the temptation would always be there, and falling would be very easy. But for now he'd managed to put not only drink, but also drugs, behind him, a major achievement. He could be open about the way he loved alcohol.

"When I hit the bottle the first time," he told *USA Today,* "I hated the taste, but the feeling was what I'd been looking for all my life."

And with sobriety came a new Ozzy. All of a sudden he had a Lifecycle, and was working out for an hour and a half every day, much to the surprise of everyone who saw him. To those who'd considered him a cartoon toward the end of the eighties—and several critics did, thinking he was more interested in the buffoonery than the music—this lean, alert Ozzy was a far cry from the man they'd known just a few years before.

HOW TO BE AN OZZY PARENT:

Stay fit so you'll be around to see your kids grow up.

On top of that, the man so famous for biting the heads off doves and bats had forsaken meat to become a vegetarian. That would waver on and off, although he'd finally become committed to that lifestyle in '97, scared by the outbreak of mad cow disease in Britain, and his own high cholesterol level. Even then, he wasn't about to become one of those who'd shout it from the rooftops and pledge undying loyalty to tofu. If he was hungry and meat was the only thing around, he'd eat it. And, he said, "I'm not like Linda McCartney and I'm not going to start making f***ing Ozzy vegetable pies. Next to Paul and Linda's stuff, fake bat burgers!"

In shape and eager to be back in the fray, he started a new decade by appearing in the video for Sam Kinison's "Under My Thumb," playing the role of the judge—something he could do quite easily, having seen a number of them in his lifetime. But more than cameo acting roles, it was music that was calling loudest to him, and he had the urge to be back on the stage, performing.

One thing no one could have anticipated was that when he returned to the stage in March, a very familiar face would be playing bass with him. Geezer Butler, his old bandmate from Sabbath, had signed on for a while, and the reunion of sorts was commemorated on *Just Say Ozzy,* a six-track live EP recorded at Brixton Academy, London. But unlike the records that had preceded it, it only made number 58 in the U.S. and number 69 in Britain. Had a renewed and revitalized Ozzy lost his audience? It was beginning to seem that way, especially as *Ten Commandments,* a collection of greatest hits released on the Priority label (and now a collector's item), barely scraped the chart at number 163.

As if waning popularity and trying to stay sober wasn't enough, Ozzy and CBS were hit by two more lawsuits, filed in Macon, Georgia. The parents of two boys who'd both killed themselves, supposedly as a result of listening to Ozzy's music (one in 1986, the other in 1988), had taken action.

In 1991, on May 6, a district court judge in Atlanta dismissed the case on First Amendment grounds. But it wasn't all laid to rest until 1992, when the Supreme Court upheld the rulings that left Ozzy protected by the First Amendment.

Ozzy himself had addressed the issue in December 1990, when speaking at the Foundation Forum's censorship panel (and who is more qualified to speak on censorship?). He noted that "if I wrote music for people who shot themselves after listening to my music, I wouldn't have much of a following"—which was an undeniable statement.

Ozzy hadn't had an album of new material since 1989, and he was eager to jump back into the saddle and see what he could do to prove wrong those who said his time at the top was over.

And so, during 1992, *No More Tears* was recorded. Some of the material had been co-written with one of rock's other great madmen, Lemmy from Motorhead, including the ballad "Mama, I'm Coming Home" (a phrase taken from calls Ozzy made to Sharon toward the end of tours), and the title cut. This was, in many ways, a newer, gentler Ozzy, and certainly there was a more thoughtful approach to the disc. "Road to Nowhere," for example, offered a very autobiographical overview of his life, and "Mr. Tinkertrain" (named for a toy store in New York) confronted child molestation issues—which was guaranteed to get Ozzy in trouble, with some groups saying that the father of five children, three of them under ten, advocated child abuse!

That was ironic; after all, this was a man who could proudly say, "we have a laugh with our kids. The hardest job in the world is being a parent, 'cause not all your decisions are the right ones. But kids ain't stupid, so don't treat them like kids. I trust my kids implicitly."

HOW TO BE AN OZZY PARENT:

Have fun with your kids.

The new Ozzy, more fun and definitely funnier, was also back in favor it seemed. His songs caught the ear of the public, and the album crashed straight into the U.S. charts at number seven, claiming the number seventeen spot in the U.K.

Ozzy Retires?

Of course, a new album meant going back out on the road. But the sober Ozzy suddenly seemed to have respect everywhere, including from the Establishment, which had previously scorned him. "I Don't Want to Change the World" received a Grammy for Best Metal Performance, a breakthrough for Ozzy. It was an irony that it had taken so long for him to receive one, since he'd practically invented the genre in the first place. But now he had it; in the eyes of music he was real, feted, and thoroughly legitimate.

But even a sober Ozzy was crazier on the road than most wasted musicians. His Theatre of Madness tour got underway, and he was determined to put on a real show for the fans. That inevitably included the "frog leaps" he'd been doing for a long time onstage—crouching like a frog and jumping. On October 26, 1991, he was performing at the Aragon Ballroom in Chicago and tried it. There shouldn't have been a problem, but he landed awkwardly, and felt something give in his foot. In fact, he'd broken it.

Being Ozzy (the man who once burned his arm with a cigarette to prove a point to a reporter), he wasn't about to let something as superficial as pain stop him, especially now that he was fit. So instead of getting the problem attended to, he simply continued with the tour, playing gigs in Cleveland, Buffalo, and the big one in New York, before he was forced to stop. His ankle had become infected, and he could hardly stand, and that meant the cancellation of the remainder of the tour, although by January, all healed, he'd be back on the road once more, in Florida, performing before a sold-out crowd of over four thousand in Sunrise.

After a brief trip to England to play a few shows there, he was back in California in March, to take part in a Randy Rhoads memorial concert in Long Beach. Ozzy dedicated the proceeds of the show to build a tomb for the man who'd been his good friend, and who'd now been dead for a decade.

Two days later, in Laguna Hills, it was back to the full-on madness, and Ozzy really should have known better. He invited the two front rows of the crowd to join him onstage, but there was no way it was ever going to be limited to that. More people—hundreds more people—crashed the stage. It got so bad that the only way Ozzy could get out was to literally get onto his knees and crawl off, escaping with some minor bruises. That left the mob to enjoy itself, and do around $100,000 in damage to the equipment and the venue.

But while most things about the tour seemed to move along with the usual craziness, there was a serious undertone. Very few knew about it, but Ozzy had been having medical problems that went beyond bruises and broken feet.

With his shuffling walk (something Ozzy had actually had for a few years), and often vacant look, as well as some numbness in his hands and feet, problems with memory, on top of reports that he'd fainted a couple of times, it had seemed that there might well be a medical condition. So Sharon had insisted on Ozzy visiting the doctor, as any wife would.

HOW TO BE AN OZZY HUSBAND:

Do what your wife tells you, if you want any peace.

Whatever she expected to hear, the result was staggering. According to the doctor, Ozzy had multiple sclerosis.

It came as a staggering blow, both to Ozzy himself and to his wife. He was forty-three, maybe old for a metal star, but still in the prime of life. He'd abused his body very heavily for more than two decades, but managed to come out the other side to sobriety. Physically, he was fitter than he'd probably ever been. He was enjoying life again. And then this had to happen.

There's no cure for MS, and its cause remains unknown. While many people still live a long time with the disease, the attacks debilitate them. In some cases, the disease can make them unable to write, read, speak, or walk. And it can kill people early.

On discovering the problem, Sharon's reaction was perfectly normal: "What the f*** am I going to do?" she wondered.

One thing was certain—the touring life, with its stresses and strains, and constant traveling, was the last thing Ozzy needed when he had MS. If anything was going to weaken him, it would be spending more years on the road. He was a family man, and his wife and kids meant the world to him. A choice between career and family was a no-brainer—family won every single time.

HOW TO BE AN OZZY PARENT:

Put your family first. Ahead of everything.

Typically, Sharon began researching the disease. She was going to have to cope with Ozzy and MS attacks, and she wanted to know what to expect. Methodical and detailed, she read books and began attending classes on how to cope with everything. On the outside she was supportive, but inside it was tearing her apart.

It was raising problems and more than a few worries for Ozzy himself, too. Dying young wasn't in his plans, not with three kids he wanted to see grow up. But he couldn't just vanish from millions of fans around the world without a word.

That was the reason for his farewell tour, going under the very apt No More Tours name. Opening June 9, 1992 in Portland, Oregon, it would run all the way until November. The reason given publicly was simply that Ozzy was retiring from the music business to spend more time with his family. And that was true, as far as it went. He would be spending more time with his family, all of his time, in fact. But there was no mention of MS in the statement. The last thing he wanted was the sympathy vote.

Ozzy's tours had always been events. This would be a *major* event. While often demonized ("It's the wonder I haven't been blamed for the outbreak of AIDS"), he could please the crowds, and this time he was selling out large venues, as fans and the curious lined up to be able to see him for one last time. But it certainly wasn't without problems. In Oklahoma City, two fans were stabbed and another twenty-nine arrested during and after the show—something Sharon blamed on the availability of alcohol at the venue (which undoubtedly raised the testosterone level in the audience to critical levels).

Perhaps the most notable part of the tour came in Texas, when Ozzy gave his first concert in San Antonio in ten years. He'd donated $10,000 to the caretakers of the Alamo as an apology for his behavior in 1982, which was enough to help them forget a wasted man in a dress and a pee stain on a wall, and the city council lifted the ban against Ozzy. After all, he wasn't going to be coming around again. However, none of that mollified San Antonio's mayor, Nelson Wolff. All he could say about the situation was, "I think it stinks."

The concert went ahead without incident.

HOW TO BE AN OZZY PARENT:

Never be afraid to say sorry.

It all wrapped up on November 14 and 15 in Costa Mesa, California, with what were billed as Ozzy's last-ever appearances (although the onstage sparkler sign that lit up and read OZZY OSBOURNE, I'LL BE BACK might have made people wonder . . .). And he pulled out all the stops. The biggest treat for fans was the surprise reunion of Black Sabbath after Ozzy had finished his own set—only Ozzy's replacement in the band, Ronnie James Dio, refused to take the stage—coming together for four classic metal songs from their repertoire: "Black Sabbath," "Iron Man," "Fairies Wear Boots," and, inevitably, the closer "Paranoid." Celebrities had crammed the place to witness the end of Ozz, ranging from Rod Stewart to Nicholas Cage, and no one went home disappointed, not even Ozzy.

But was he really gone? You wouldn't have thought so, even though he said, "Who wants to be touring at forty-six? I screwed all the groupies when it was safe . . . It's time to go home." A couple of days after his "final" appearance he was putting his hands in wet concrete for the cameras as Black Sabbath received their star on the Rock Walk on Sunset Boulevard in Hollywood. He'd literally cemented his fame at last.

There had to be a souvenir of this last tour, of course, and it appeared in July 1993, a double set called, aptly, *Live and Loud,* which was actually combined from the No More Tours and Theatre of Madness tours. It peaked at number twenty-two, but still managed to go gold in just over a month, no mean achievement.

Back in England, Ozzy was supposed to be living the easy life, enjoying his family and resting. But one thing he couldn't resist was a chance to appear on a religious program broadcast by the

BBC, *Faith and Music,* which aired—to numerous protests—in
May 1993.

One thing he wasn't going to do was let the disease beat him.
Being healthy and fit was a key to keeping it at bay, and now that he
was sober, he could put himself wholeheartedly into that. "I started
working out—it's the greatest stress release in the world. I love
working out. I love breaking a sweat. If I don't work out at least
once a day, it affects my mood and my day. And," he admitted can-
didly, "it is another addiction. I mean, I am an addictive person, so
anything I like will be an addiction."

It was typical, perfect Ozzy. Never do anything by half-measures.

He became, according to Sharon, a hypochondriac. "He likes to
think he's sick all the time and he likes to go to doctors to get more
drugs."

"I am addicted to pills and medication," Ozzy agreed. And he
had a list of prescribed medications he was taking that would have
toppled most people. "But I don't get stoned on these pills," he was
quick to add. "Believe me, if I did there wouldn't be a pill left in
the bottle. I'd be lying on the floor with a f***ing funnel in my
mouth."

None of that halted the specter of MS, however. It seemed
inevitable that sooner or later there'd be a physical decline leading
to death—hardly happy thoughts. So far, though, he was holding
his own far better than the doctor had expected. That was a relief
for the family, although the various medications he was taking produced their own peculiar side effects: for example, his antipsy-
chotic medicine (something some people believed he should have
been taking for years) gave him the kind of tremors in his hands

and legs often seen in people suffering from Parkinson's disease (which has touched actor Michael J. Fox). It led to a rumor that Ozzy was suffering from Parkinson's, which was quite untrue.

Curiously, one thing Sharon had never done was get a second opinion on Ozzy's condition. Perhaps surprisingly, she'd simply accepted the first diagnosis she'd been given. Or perhaps she'd been so stunned by the finality of it that it seemed as if another opinion would be a waste of time.

While it kept Ozzy off the road and out of the studio, his supposed illness didn't seem to have slowed him down at all. He still took part in *Halloween Jam II,* taped at Universal Studios, attended the Grammy Awards, and was presented with the *Kerrang!* Kudos Award in June 1994. He also found time to record a duet with Miss Piggy (of Steppenwolf's classic rock anthem, "Born to be Wild") on *Kermit Unplugged*. It was hardly total retirement, not when his face appeared in the media every few months, looking thinner, fitter, and more rested than ever before.

He and Sharon even attended one of America's biggest social events of 1994, the New York wedding of singer Mariah Carey to her label boss, CBS head Tommy Mottola. Ozzy still recorded for CBS, and had been a consistently high-selling act.

At the reception, Sharon and Mottola began talking about Ozzy's illness, which still hadn't become public news. He suggested she seek a second opinion, and that was what she did—in fact a second and third opinion.

One of the doctors was quite forthright. As soon as he saw Ozzy shuffle into his office, he began to laugh.

"He hasn't got MS, he's just f***ing stoned!" was the verdict.

And the tests showed he was right. Ozzy wasn't suffering from MS at all, and never had been. A weight was lifted from the entire Osbourne family. Suddenly they realized the pressure they'd been living under for two years. It was like having a death sentence lifted.

HOW TO BE AN OZZY PARENT:

Live every day as if it was your last.

But it did raise a problem. Ozzy had retired because he was ill. Now that he was no longer ill, what the hell was he going to do?

Retirement for its own sake didn't sit well with him. He wasn't made to simply sit around for the rest of his life, even though he did enjoy it for short periods. But he'd said he was out of the business.

". . . We'd already announced the big farewell and it was really embarrassing," Sharon recalled in 2001. "We just had to go, 'Only joking!' Ten years on we can laugh about it, but it was a hard, terrible time."

Certainly, coming back wouldn't be easy. In some ways it would be a betrayal, and while Ozzy had done a lot of things in his life, he'd always respected his fans. To be sure, if he did stage a comeback, there'd be people who'd think the retirement had just been a ploy to get people to buy albums and see his show. And that simply wasn't the way he operated.

There was another factor, too. He'd been out of the public eye for a couple of years, and in rock terms that was close to a lifetime. There were new metal gods now, acts like Metallica (whom Ozzy had had as a support band as early as 1983) and the grunge acts like Soundgarden. They'd taken over the airwaves, the concert halls, and MTV, which had itself become the arbiter of America's musical taste. What guarantee was there that Ozzy would even have a place anymore? His own fans were getting older, and it was the younger ones who really went to shows and bought CDs.

"F*** MTV," Ozzy said in 1995. "I always remember long careers being built by word of mouth . . . I mean, you think back to the mid eighties, when there were the Poisons and the Cinderellas and all these f***ing bands selling millions of records, and I'm going, 'F*** me, how am I going to survive this?' Well, here I am, still going strong."

But he couldn't get over the fact that he hated retirement. He loved his family, and he still did things, but he was bored. Making music was what he did, the only job he'd done for any length of time. And he wanted to do it again.

He'd begun writing with one of the hottest guitarists around, Steve Vai, and there were persistent rumors of them starting a band together. That wouldn't happen, but one of their collaborations, "My Little Man," which was written for Jack Osbourne, would at least be recorded with Vai playing guitar.

Ozzy was ready to unleash his next salvo on the world. Retirement was over. He went back into the studio with Geezer back on bass and Dean Castronovo on drums. The plan had been for some tracks to feature Vai on guitar, and others to have Zakk Wylde back again. Wylde was unable to commit to the entire album because, having taken Ozzy's retirement seriously (which it was at the time), he was busy with his own band, Pride and Glory.

Recording took place in Paris, with Michael Beinhorn behind the boards, and it felt good to be back.

"There was no inspiration or direction," Ozzy said of the record, "my band from before disbanded, I put together not so much a band as a group of songwriters. There were so many mellow songs on the album, it lacked a couple of rockers. I've never acknowledged alternative, or metal, or anything, it's just an Ozzy album, or what you might think of as an Ozzy alternative album. If you like it, you like it."

"One thing about this record is that you're never short of a surprise," he added about the disc that would be called *Ozzmosis*. "And every time you put a new album out, it's like gambling on the Grand National . . . But for me it's been like a gestation period— only it's a three-year pregnancy! I've never spent so much time and money on an album in my life."

A new album meant a new tour, because if there was anyplace that Ozzy came alive, it was onstage. Geezer and Dean were in, but Vai wasn't, and, it transpired, neither was Zakk Wylde.

According to some, Wylde was also negotiating with Guns N' Roses to join them, so Ozzy began auditioning new guitar players for the band. Then Wylde's manager called Sharon to say he was available, although Wylde himself said he was still negotiating with Guns N' Roses. Ozzy needed to know what was happening. He called Wylde, but when his call wasn't returned, he went ahead and replaced the man who'd worked with him for most of his solo career.

The person he found actually kept the extended family connection going. Joe Holmes had been a student of Randy Rhoads's at the beginning of the eighties. He'd played with David Lee Roth, so he came with credentials. Ozzy was certainly impressed by the new addition, saying, "The one regret I do have is not finding Joe before *Ozzmosis,* because it would have been a nice way to launch off."

Perhaps oddly, Ozzy didn't kick things off in America, opting instead to begin in Mexico and then head farther south, headlining the Monsters of Rock tour, with Alice Cooper, Megadeth, Paradise Lost, and Therapy?.

One thing Ozzy planned on was giving fans value for their money, turning in sets that averaged two hours, and covered not only the new material, but also plenty of old favorites. Holmes fitted in well, and Butler was an old hand who was perfectly relaxed on the road, but Castronovo quit after just a few shows, to be replaced by the returning Randy Castillo. As an added bonus, there was a Black Sabbath medley as part of the music, guaranteed to please all Ozzy fans (and he carried on playing it, even after Butler left in December 1995, homesick for England).

By Ozzy's previous standards, it was a strange band indeed. No one drank, there were no drugs. It was a very new experience. But just because this was a new Ozzy, that didn't mean he was any less fun. He'd discovered the simple, wet pleasures of the supersoaker water guns. About the only problem was that the tank on them didn't last long or go too far from the stage. But with a few modifications, Ozzy started his new tradition of soaking audiences, which he does to this day—although the machinery has gotten much bigger and better over the years, and the jets of water far more powerful.

According to Ozzy, "I think it was my wife," who began it all. "It started off with a bottle of water one time, then a bucket, and then somebody came up with the supersoakers. It's just good fun, you know. It's kind of become the new Ozzy trademark, now."

HOW TO BE AN OZZY PARENT:

You can enjoy good clean fun.

The shows gathered rave reviews, and members of various bands came close to being arrested for indecent exposure and several other things.

Latin America proved to be a good warm-up for Ozzy and the band before heading back north to take on America. That would be the big test, to see if he could still be accepted and still sell tickets in the U.S. But with the strong bill, containing a range of older and younger bands, there was a wide appeal. And the American jaunt was very short, a kind of toe in the water to see if the fan base was still there.

Judging by the fact that *Ozzmosis* crashed onto the chart at number four without the help of MTV, it was evident people still loved

CLASSIC OZZY SONG TITLES

"Diary of a Madman"

"Bark at the Moon"

"Waiting for Darkness"

"Devil's Daughter"

"Bloodbath in Paradise"

"Demon Alcohol"

"Zombie Stomp"

"Road to Nowhere"

"See You on the Other Side"

"My Jekyll Doesn't Hide"

"Facing Hell"

Ozzy. He was sticking to smaller venues, however, the reason being, he said, "I wanted to start out small, and put the word out, and I am on the road for the duration and I will never retire again."

He had done one video, for the single "Perry Mason" (which made the U.K. charts, as did the album), but it wasn't a priority with him. Recording and touring were what mattered, in particular touring, because "I realized where I belonged."

And the introduction to his stage performance these days was a video, a kind of *Forrest Gump* affair that magically slotted Ozzy next to famous musical, political, and historical figures. It was far from serious—which summed up the man himself, really—and made a perfect opening to an over-the-top affair.

"There are a bunch of versions of it. My wife said she was considering putting it and a bunch of other stuff never released together to release . . . it's hilarious, and it was a lot of fun to do, as well. All in all I think we've got about an hour of stuff."

Playing live revitalized him, especially when he began the European leg of the tour in Britain, although a couple of shows had to be canceled, first when Castillo came down with carpal tunnel syndrome, and then when Ozzy himself suffered laryngitis—one of the few times in his life when he had nothing to say!

He was working almost until Christmas itself, filming a video on the twenty-third, before heading back to the farm. Then, according to his diary, "It's Christmas Eve and the house is full of excitement. It's really nice and cold and feeling very Christmasy. We went out for a late dinner and then went to midnight mass at our local church."

The idea of Ozzy at midnight mass—as opposed to a midnight

black mass—might have surprised a few people, but offstage he'd truly become a complete family man, spending as much time at home as he possibly could, and loving just being around his wife and kids.

HOW TO BE AN OZZY PARENT:

Remember Christmas is for kids.

And the next day it was back on the road. No rest for the wicked, even if they'd long since given up most of the wickedness. The family did join him for some American dates, in between some skiing in Vail. As a New Year's resolution, Ozzy had quit smoking for the first time in his life, and the withdrawal symptoms were driving him crazy.

While Ozzy's kids were a good bunch, they really wouldn't have been his offspring if they didn't have at least some mischief in their genes. And they showed it on a plane trip, where Ozzy was suffering through nicotine withdrawal, wearing, he claimed, Nicoderm patches all over his face.

"Unbeknownst to me, there are two women sitting behind me on the plane who kept talking about me the entire flight. My kids overheard them and got p***ed off. They found out where one of their coats were hanging and put their dinner in her coat pocket. Shrimp tails, chicken bones, some half-eaten mashed potatoes and peas all went in the coat pocket."

OZZY'S FIVE MOST OUTRAGEOUS STUNTS

Arrested for burglary. He knew that if he wore gloves he wouldn't leave fingerprints; however, he wore fingerless gloves.

Biting the head off a dove in front of representatives of his new American record company.

Biting the head off a bat while onstage.

Pissing on the greatest historical landmark in Texas, the Alamo, while wearing his wife's evening dress.

Snorting a line of ants as if they were cocaine.

Revenge, as they say, is a dish best served cold, and someone would get the surprise of some very cold food later . . .

Ozzy persisted with quitting smoking, substituting food for cigarettes. However, he was putting on a pound a day (no small amount), which wasn't the kind of news he wanted to hear. Even working out regularly didn't help.

Still, he did surprisingly well, lasting into February, and toughing it out for over a month. But on February 12, 1996, he began smoking again.

From time to time, the family would pop up on the tour, which brought both joys and drawbacks.

"My plane has now turned into a mobile toy store. The plane only seats eight and four of the seats are crammed with toys. I spent the entire journey picking Legos out of my a**. The show was really fun tonight. I love it when my kids are on the road with me and I look over during the show and see them on the side of the stage."

However youthful and playful Ozzy seemed, however, there were times when his age was inevitably bound to catch up with him, as it did it when he slipped on one of Jack's toys in the bathtub and threw his back out.

And *that* was just the start. By the time he reached California, he was genuinely sick, to the point where he had to be hospitalized for a few days, slowly getting back to normal only by the time the band reached Japan, where "I've now taken to wearing a surgical mask and gloves when I travel. I feel like Michael Jackson's ugly brother." However, it was a necessary precaution given the number of people Ozzy encountered every day. "And if one of those people have got the shits, or the flu, or bronchitis, or are on their period, or pregnant, I'm gonna catch it off them. I'm not gonna let it happen again! So you can all f***ing laugh, I don't f***ing care."

But once Japan was finished, it was back to the U.S. and a return to normalcy (or as normal as an Ozzy tour could ever be), with a lot more dates, making Ozzy's comeback a major event—although never-ending to him. The monotony of the road wore him down now that he was sober, although he generally coped well with it. At times, however, craziness did set in, and he had to do *something*, such as when he found a tattoo artist in the Yellow Pages and had new art put on his right arm. "I have no idea what the f*** it is, but it took him about seven hours the first day to get it started. I think I'm happy with it, but I'll have to wait until it's finished."

Ozzy had come back in a big way, and having bands like the up-and-coming Korn on the bill helped him reach a new audience. And he was a hit with kids to whom he'd just been a name before. Even if Ozzy sometimes used a TelePrompTer to remember his lyrics, they loved him.

HOW TO BE AN OZZY PARENT:

Keep your mind young.

That gave Sharon an idea. If Ozzy could get more exposure to a younger crowd, he could find a whole new audience, which would help prolong his career, since, effectively, his core crowd was getting older.

She had no doubt that Ozzy was cool enough, but others seemed a lot less certain. After all, he was close to fifty now, so how could that fit in with much younger musicians, even if they'd grown up listening to his music? On the basis of his last tour, it would work very well. And Ozzy was certainly ready for more gigs. After three years off the road, he was greedy for as much of it as he could get now. Despite the illnesses of touring, he was happy to be back in his home away from home, however grueling it might be.

Sharon was looking around for opportunities for Ozzy. After all, he'd released the most impressive album of his long career, he was performing better than ever, and she knew the time was right to make Ozzy larger than he'd ever been. The only thing she needed was for someone else to agree with her and help it happen.

Ozzfest

In many ways, the credit for Ozzfest, Ozzy's annual touring extravaganza, goes to Lollapalooza. That festival, put together by Perry Ferrell of Jane's Addiction, had become *the* showcase for alternative bands in the early nineties. It was also extremely profitable, a feast of bands and sideshows that traveled across America every summer.

To Sharon Osbourne, it seemed like the perfect venue to expose her husband to a young audience, and bring him a whole new core of fans that would sustain him for many years to come.

So she approached the organizers of Lollapalooza. She claimed that they turned Ozzy down because they believed a forty-seven-year-old rock star simply wasn't right enough for their show.

"They laughed at the idea," she recalls, eyes burning at the injustice. "They all thought Ozzy was so uncool. So I thought, 'Right, I'll organize my own fucking festival.'"

Not a woman to be trifled with, that was exactly what she did. A famous, even revered figure in the metal music business, she quickly put together a lineup of sixteen bands, and arranged two dates, in Phoenix and San Bernadino, that both sold out immediately. And so the beast known as Ozzfest was born.

For Ozzy, the success was a vindication of his popularity. "... Some f***ing d*** said to me, 'Don't you think a forty-seven-year-old man is a bit too old to be doing this?' He didn't know what he was f***ing talking about."

It wasn't just a good move, it was also very intelligently put together. While there were some huge metal names on the bill— alongside Ozzy there were Slayer and Sepultura, for example— there were also many younger bands, like Fear Factory and Biohazard to draw in the younger fans.

There was never any doubt about Ozzy, armed with his super-soaker water gun, being the headlining act. And of course there was also the sideshow atmosphere, where people attending could not only buy food, clothes, and other merchandise, but also get a tattoo or a piercing, or watch men put drills up their noses.

It was a major winner, confounding every expectation that metal was largely dead. But Sharon Osbourne had always been a woman to back winners—or to take people and make them into winners. And with this new franchise, she was obviously onto something good.

Still, she couldn't have been Ozzy's wife without displaying a slightly evil sense of humor, and it came to the fore in California, or at least it attempted to. Evidently, on the Phoenix date, Glenn Danzig of Danzig had allegedly smashed the official festival photographer's camera during his set, which didn't make Sharon a happy camper. As revenge, she planned to set up the video cameras to show Danzig's rumored bald patch and chubby waistline. And, impishly, she'd also hoped to distribute free disposable cameras to everyone in the front row—a plan thwarted only by not being able to get as many cameras as she wanted.

"The Ozzfest was a real gamble that worked," said Ozzy. "I'd have looked pretty stupid if no one had turned up."

It's interesting that over the years Ozzfest has grown from its two-date beginning, a tentative start, into a huge event that spends much of the summer on the road, and that Lollapalooza, the festival which refused Ozzy, has been dead for several years—in much the same way that alternative music died. And Ozzy helped put the stake through its heart when he teamed up with Type O Negative, a band not known for its subtlety, to perform a version of the old Status Quo hit, "Pictures of Matchstick Men" for the movie *Howard Stern's Private Parts* (in which Ozzy also had a cameo acting role, padding out his movie resume).

Without setting out to do so, Sharon had created a brand-new monster—the touring metal festival. Of course, the fact that it had worked once didn't mean it would necessarily work again. But Ozzy would be touring regardless, so it simply made sense to try and make another Ozzfest work. The trick would be to offer people something that would make them flock in and see the festival, something they simply couldn't see anywhere else.

What better way to draw in a crowd than to give them a reunion of Black Sabbath? Now *that* would be something to bring them through the turnstiles.

But could it be done after almost twenty years, and plenty of acrimony? Granted, Geezer had often played with Ozzy during the nineties, and they remained good friends, but Ozzy and Tony had rarely had anything good to say about each other during the intervening years.

"I don't think we've ever been enemies," Iommi countered. "Whatever has been made out in the past—and that's all water under the bridge—we were in contact with each other, one way or another."

HOW TO BE AN OZZY PARENT:

Tell your kids to keep the friends of their youth.

The simple fact was that the rest of Sabbath weren't doing anywhere near as well as Ozzy in terms of career. He'd come back from retirement stronger than ever, a powerful force on the scene, especially in America. They seemed to be slowly becoming musical fossils, all of them mostly pursuing individual paths.

Bringing back Black Sabbath was something that appealed to them all. Enough time had passed since Ozzy was fired in 1979 that history had become ancient. "To be honest, I find that a lot of press people are fishing for things, like 'You said this about Iommi,' or 'Iommi said this about you.' Whether I did or whether I didn't doesn't matter. It was a long time ago. Get over it. For f***'s sake, if that was the case, nobody would speak to anyone who was f***ing German because of the war."

And more important, all four members were sober now, which helped. As Iommi noted when they did regroup, "If we had been here twenty-eight years ago, we'd be sitting here as p***ed as rats. One of us would be spewing over in the corner."

While hardly painting a pretty picture, he was right. But now, said Ozzy, "we're in a different state of mind." They'd all grown up, they were older and wiser, and able to joke about all the craziness they'd gone through.

The time was right, the world was waiting; they were going to do it.

They would be the cornerstone of the 1997 Ozzfest in the U.S.

From the time they got back together, it felt perfect. But they'd all come up together, they'd done drugs together, got drunk together, experienced the road together. Even after so long apart, they knew each other well. They were the godfathers of metal. And they were going to show all the young pretenders what it was about.

"It's only in the last ten years that we've realized what kind of an impact we've had," said Ozzy.

"With the whole grunge thing, those guys gave credit to Sabbath," said Ward. "That was like a 'thank you' for all the years that we'd put in."

Ward, however, wasn't involved initially in the reunion.

"When the idea to put the original band back together came about," Geezer remembered, "Ozzy called me and Tony up and said, 'This has got to be a yes or a no situation—there can't be a maybe because the Ozzfest is being booked. When it came to Bill, we didn't know what to do. We couldn't say we were getting back together just to have him pull out again. We thought we'd test the water and, if it didn't work, at least we could say it was only three of us!"

According to Ward, however, "Everybody in the band knew where I lived, everybody had my phone number, but nobody bothered to use it. I think the deal was that they said, 'Let's try it without Bill.' That's okay."

And so, with a different drummer behind the kit, they settled down for rehearsals. For Ozzy, the tour was going to be crazy and grueling. Not only would he be performing as part of Sabbath, who were the headlining act across the U.S., he'd also be appearing fronting his own band, playing two full sets a night. It would require plenty of stamina, although neither band would be putting in the two-hour efforts he'd done on the *Ozzmosis* jaunt.

Once again, it was a huge bill, combining talents old and new, enough to satisfy even the most critical metal fan. And the tantalizing prospect of seeing Black Sabbath, heroes to a generation— maybe even two generations by now—of music makers was something wonderful.

It was exactly the kind of ticket Sharon needed to establish the festival as a real entity, and it was likely to be one of the biggest draws of the summer season. Certainly the fact that the dates sold out immediately was enough to indicate the success. With the more underground bands relegated to the second stage, there was plenty of musical choice—including someone who had taken Ozzy's place as the Antichrist in the eyes of the Christian right— Marilyn Manson.

HOW TO BE AN OZZY PARENT:

Tell your kids never to judge a book by its cover.

Many of the bands had returned from the year before, happy with the experience and excited to have the chance to actually see Sabbath perform. Many of them would gather at the side of the stage every night to bang their heads to Sabbath playing a fifty-minute set with drummer Mike Bordin, from Faith No More, who'd also just finished a set behind Ozzy, on drums. In fact, Ozzfest '97 remains the overwhelming favorite among fans, with 63 percent voting for it, far more than any other—the next closest is '99, with just 27 percent of the vote.

To coincide with the festival, Ozzy's brand new label, Ozz Records, issued its first CD, a compilation of bands who'd been on Ozzfest '96. That meant Ozzy was more than a rock star now, he was becoming a corporation and a franchise, thanks not only to his own talent and longevity, but also to Sharon, who'd carefully organized the business side of things to make this happen. Not only was this all fabulous exposure for Ozzy, better than he could ever have received from the fading Lollapalooza, but it was also proving remarkably lucrative. Bands truly wanted to be a part of it. And with the crowds packing it in at every venue, it was beginning to seem like a license to print money (and it's one reason why the Osbournes are worth over $58 million today).

It was the perfect time for Ozzy to release a *Best Of* CD, this one going under the title of *The Ozzman Cometh*. But it was really more than just his best-known songs. Spread over two discs, it included four early Sabbath demos (with appalling sound quality!), a brand-new Ozzy track, "Back to Earth," in addition to all kinds of multimedia toys, such as screen savers, games, and movies. In other words, it was exactly what Ozzy himself might have wanted if he'd been buying a greatest hits—all the stuff and more.

The way Ozzfest had taken off also made the couple think about a few things. They loved England, but America was where they did most of their work, and made most of their income. There was really nothing to stop them from moving to the U.S. and setting up a home there. It would be good for them, and it would also be good for the children to grow up in the sun. They'd always liked Los Angeles. And it wasn't as if America was unfamiliar territory—they'd all spent plenty of time in Vail, Colorado, New York, and L.A. And in L.A., the capital of movies and television, everyone was crazy, anyway—Ozzy could feel right at home.

The three-quarters Sabbath reunion had been great, and very well received. People wanted to see them—people *really* wanted to see them. And that didn't mean just in America. They had to take their show to England, and bring it home.

But, realistically, there was no way to do that without Bill Ward on drums. He was contacted, and agreed to play. This was the *real* Sabbath, ready to set heads banging. They'd arranged two special reunion concerts in their hometown of Birmingham for December 4 and 5, 1997, which would be recorded for future release (in fact, the album would appear at the same time as the video of the show).

"Over the years, I've had various lineups covering Sabbath classics like 'Iron Man,' 'Paranoid,' 'War Pigs,' and the rest," Ozzy mused. "And they've all been good players, but it's nothing like the real thing."

The Birmingham shows were both sellouts, and a huge success. To English ears the band sounded better than they ever had in their heyday. In fact, Ozzy considered the second night to be in the top twenty shows he'd played in his life, high praise from someone who was playing so many dates each year. There was no doubt that, having come back, Ozzy was making the most of being out of retirement.

According to the review in *MOJO,* there was "lovable Ozzy, scampering around like a four-year-old, clapping his hands and stomping on the spot like a Duracell bunny, waving his hands from side to side, exhorting us all to 'go f***ing crazy.' "

HOW TO BE AN OZZY PARENT:

If you have fun in your own life, you can bring it to others.

Something all the Sabbath members wanted to do was go back on the road and bring their music to a new generation around the world. With the days of madness behind them all, perhaps the time was right. They'd conquered a two-hour set, far more than they'd ever had to play back in their prime, and come out with flying colors.

GREAT SABBATH MOMENTS

At one gig, the head of the Hell's Angels turned up. "About fifty bodyguards came in first," recalled Geezer. "Then he told us who he was, and that we'd be all right wherever we go—whatever that meant. They stayed and watched the show and then they went—in a big motorcycle cavalcade."

Ozzy found a groupie lying on the floor of his hotel bar. Thinking she was sick, he tried to help her stand up. She screamed, and he tried again, only to have her scream louder. "I thought she was having a fit," he said, "until she said, 'You're standing on my f***ing hair!' "

After one show, they were met by a group of Satanists in their hotel corridor, clutching black candles and chanting. The band blew out the candles and began singing "Happy Birthday." "They got pissed off, they just left!"

When Black Sabbath made the album chart in England, "My knees went to jelly, I was speechless," said Ozzy. "I couldn't f***ing believe it! From that moment on, my life totally went off like a rocket."

So take it on the road was exactly what they decided to do, on a European tour that included the first U.K. Ozzfest. It was a metal fan's dream come true. Not only was there Sabbath and Ozzy at Ozzfest, but also the Foo Fighters, the band begun by former Nirvana drummer Dave Grohl, Ozzfest regulars Pantera, and many more.

Lollapalooza had never ventured outside the U.S., and now Ozzy was winning over the U.K. and he was proud of it. "In 1996, when we did the first Ozzfest in America, people were saying that we were out of our minds—that nobody would care about a heavy music festival. Well, we ended up selling fifty thousands tickets over two gigs. And last summer, we kicked the a** of every other festival that was touring the U.S. When you come to the Ozzfest, it's like a party from beginning to end."

And that was what they brought to the Milton Keynes Bowl. A party that seemed like it was never going to stop. And if Ozzy had anything to do with it, it never would stop. Ever.

He was lucky, and he realized it. Back in Birmingham he'd run into old school friends who now had beer bellies, were bald, and had mortgages. They looked beaten down by life, where Ozzy felt as if he was just getting into his stride. He was living life on his own terms—even if he'd changed the terms from when he was young.

There was no shortage of people ready and willing to work with Ozzy. The success of Ozzfest had made him a hot property. Not that he'd been cold before, that much was obvious, but now he was sizzling like never before in his career. He teamed up with rapper Busta Rhymes to cover "Iron Man" as a rap, then contributed a

song to the *South Park* soundtrack, working with rappers DMX and
Ol' Dirty Bastard, along with Crystal Method.

Then it was time for the third Ozzfest, during the month of July
1998. Sharon understood well enough that it made more sense not
to do a long string of dates around the country, but to have the festival in focal points that would bring in people from a region. It
helped drive up the profits. And once again, she put together a
shrewd bill. Of course, Ozzy was the headliner, as always, supported
by acts like Motorhead, Megadeth, Tool, and Limp Bizkit—the mix
of the old and the new that had worked so well for the last two
years.

And once again, Ozzfest came up a winner. The crowds flocked
in, everyone had a great time, and it raked in money, hand over
fist. There was certainly never any doubt that it would be returning
for as long as people were interested, and now that it had been a
success in England, too, it was vastly extending its scope.

Between that and a Sabbath tour, Ozzy was set for yet another
busy year. But then, except for his time in retirement, every year
had been busy.

But the Sabbath tour almost became a nonstarter. The newly
returned Ward suffered a heart attack, and was forced to drop out
of the planned dates. It wasn't life-threatening, but enough to
make him realize he needed a rest. Vinny Appice, another former
Sabbath drummer, took over the seat behind the kit for the tour.
Perhaps it didn't make for the perfect reunion, but health came
before everything else, as Ozzy himself had learned in the past.
Luckily, it was just a short tour before Ozzfest kicked off in the
U.S.—and this year Sabbath wasn't going to be a part of it.

ABOVE. *Just out with the kids* (AFP/Corbis)

LEFT. *Ozzy wishes for some peace at the White House Correspondents' Dinner, Washington D.C., May 2002.* (AFP/Corbis)

Ozzy, 1983. A star then, a star still. (Roger Ressmeyer/Corbis)

ABOVE. *Just when you thought it was safe to go in the water...* (S.I.N./Corbis)

BELOW. *Back when they were babies—Ozzy and Sharon with Aimee and newborn Kelly, 1984* (Neal Preston/Corbis)

Jack announces the lineup for Ozzfest 2002. (Spencer Platt/Getty Images)

Finally, a star! Ozzy at the Hollywood Walk of Fame. (Vince Bucci/Getty Images)

ABOVE. *Ozzy and Sharon announce a second season for* The Osbournes *on* The Tonight Show with Jay Leno, *May 2002.*
(NBC/Getty Images)

BELOW. *Ozzy displays some of his tattoos.* (Chris Felver/Getty Images)

Ozzy, the king of Ozzfest 2000 (George DeSota/Getty Images)

A kiss for Sharon (AFP/Corbis)

However, they were far from gone again. In September, the *Reunion* CD and video appeared, with an added attraction, even for those who'd seen the Birmingham concerts—there were two new album cuts, the first issued by the original lineup since 1979, almost two decades before. "Psycho Man" and "Selling My Soul" had been recorded in Wales, and had all the power of the best of Sabbath's material, even if they weren't as well known.

The reality was that they were having too much fun to let the idea of a reborn Sabbath end. Beyond Ozzfest, America hadn't had an opportunity to see the band, so they planned an American tour, which began on New Year's Eve, 1998, and would last until February. However, there were a number of cancellations, mostly due to throat problems Ozzy was having—in fact, the entire last four dates ended up not happening, and were never made up.

There was also plenty of talk about a new Sabbath album with the "proper" lineup, although the world is still waiting to hear it. More important by far, however, was the touring. However, the question was, what could they do? Ozzy couldn't really carry on two careers, and the others had interests outside Sabbath—solo albums to make.

And so they decided to make 1999 the last year of Sabbath. Twenty years since they'd broken up. For Ward, who'd reclaimed his drum stool after recovering from the heart attack, "it was difficult for me to accept that a decision has been made to stop. I respect that decision, but right now it's hard to come to terms with it. I'd like to continue because I think this band sounds incredibly good right now."

Billing it as "The Last Supper," Sabbath was ready for what

would amount to a seven-month tour. First would come Ozzfest, then the final celebration around the globe, culminating in two more shows, the last ever, in their hometown to round things off.

For Ozzy, he didn't want "to see Sabbath get dragged down and down," the way it had before. "I'd rather end it on a high note. If we ever get together again after this, at least we can start again on a high note."

But there was never any danger of them going out on anything less than a high note. This was the big bang, the last supper, after which there'd be no dessert. At the same time, Ozzy wasn't closing the door on anything in the future.

HOW TO BE AN OZZY PARENT:

Tell your kids never to burn their bridges—
they might want to cross them again.

For the month of June, they shared the stage with the likes of Rob Zombie, Slayer, the Deftones, and Godsmack, as the festival wended its way across the U.S. But even after that was done, there was no rest for the wicked, even if they didn't have the inclination to be anywhere near as wicked as they used to be.

As Ozzfest packed up and went home, much richer, and with another year under its belt, the Last Supper tour continued, playing to packed houses, until they finished in August at Jones Beach in New York. America could be checked off their list.

SHARON AT HER BEST

She paid her father, Don Arden, $1.5 million to get Ozzy's contract and become his manager. Since then she's never spoken to him.

She quit managing the alternative band Smashing Pumpkins, announcing that she was leaving "for medical reasons—Billy Corgan was making me sick!"

She allegedly once kneed a promoter in the groin when he was a little recalcitrant about paying.

She threw a whole ham over the hedge into her neighbors' yard to complain about them playing music too loud.

She went to the office of a company producing illegal Ozzy merchandise and trashed their computer system. Then she had to go back, because she'd left her car keys there.

She had Ozzy arrested in 1989 for trying to kill her—but later dropped the charges. They're still together, celebrating their twentieth anniversary on July 4, 2002.

When Ozzy was once denounced by a fundamentalist preacher as "a practicing cannibal," she answered, "That's about the one thing Ozzy hasn't done."

But after a break of a couple of months, it was a case of packing everything in the trucks again, and heading out across Europe for what would *really* be the last hurrah. There were shows in London, through Germany, Finland, and Sweden, before heading home to Birmingham to close it all out on the highest note they could find.

It was a far cry from the Sabbath of old. No drugs, no drinking. None of them even smoked a cigarette during their European tour, as sober as they could possibly be. But even though Ozzy had managed to put drink and illegal drugs behind him, that didn't mean he wasn't tempted.

"I've given it up but *it* hasn't," he explained. "It's waiting there going 'Just one drag or one little vat won't hurt you.' It always does it at night. I end up talking to it going. 'Shut the f*** up!' Sharon said to me the other day, 'I'm a bit worried about you, you've started talking to yourself.' I said, 'So? I'm a f***ing nutter!' I end up shouting things like 'Die!' 'Not now!' or 'F*** off!' She thinks I'm going round the bend when I'm just talking to this thing in my head."

It was pure Ozzy. This was the man who tried to confuse the little man in his head by thinking that he could have a drink if he wanted it. And when the voice asked if he wanted a drink after all, he'd answer, "No, f*** off."

HOW TO BE AN OZZY PARENT:

Tell your kids never to obey the voices in their heads.

There was a logic to it that made perfect sense in Ozzy's world. Often that world overlapped with the real world, especially when it involved music. And at other times it seemed to be a place only he could inhabit. The bottom line, however, was that he'd managed to stay sober for a long time, his system was clean, he remained fit and active, and he was probably playing more music than he ever had before.

Still, even though they thought they'd rounded things off, it transpired that they hadn't. On February 23, 2000, Black Sabbath received a Grammy for "Iron Man," off *Reunion,* which had been voted Best Metal Performance. Standing on the stage, wearing an expensive suit, Bill Ward said, "I think it's totally cool . . . I didn't think that thirty-one years ago, I'd be standing up in a suit. I feel more like an accountant than the guy who plays drums in Black Sabbath."

By then the specter of the millennium had come and gone, without any of the major catastrophes that had been predicted.

Ozzy's advice for the witching hour, as the century ended was, "Have a wank, because it's a good laugh. If this really is the end of the world, then I want to go spanking Frank. It'll be a case of come as you go!"

So was it the end for Sabbath? Could the lads really let it rest, had they had enough of each other to last them the rest of their lives? While no one had been saying never again, every indication had been that way, even if no tempers were frayed or fists raised. The much-discussed album had never appeared, and since the final concerts everyone had been quiet.

Except Ozzy, of course. The road maniac was back on tour

again, as if it was a drug he couldn't live without. And maybe that was what it was all about—another, less lethal, addiction. It might have been taxing, but he loved it. And he loved his time away from the road, too, even though most of his year seemed to be spent traveling.

When he was invited to play a summer show for radio station KROQ in Los Angeles, everyone expected Ozzy to show up with his own band. And that would have been fine—that was who they booked. Instead, he took them all by surprise when the four people who emerged from the limo turned out to be Ozzy, Tony, Geezer, and Bill. Yes, Sabbath was back. Again.

HOW TO BE AN OZZY PARENT:

Surprise parties are fun.

Perhaps it was an omen, though, that the rotating stage they were using for their show didn't exactly work as planned. During the very first number, it managed to cut all the power wires, causing a ten-minute delay as roadies hastily patched cables together before the riffage could start in earnest. The badly behaved prop also caused the cancellation of another Sabs show in New Jersey a week later.

One thing the terrible foursome wouldn't be doing, however, was Ozzfest. That had already been settled, and the festival was going out with a bigger bill than ever, as a total of eighteen bands took to the road together in a carnival-like atmosphere.

While Ozzy was, as always, the headliner, Ozzfest was as much Sharon's show as his. She was not only the coordinator; she looked after the bands and clucked around them, doing things like ordering a musician to see a doctor in order to have his bronchitis treated. And they appreciated the attention she gave them all. She'd become a metal den mother, and it did matter—one musician even brought her a thank-you note from his mother, who appreciated her son's band being on the tour!

By now the family had settled into Los Angeles, making Malibu their home when they weren't on a plane or a bus. Sharon and the kids often toured with Ozzy. By now Aimee, Jack, and Kelly were teenagers, aware of themselves, and quite capable of getting into trouble away from parental supervision (during Ozzfest 2000, Jack would get his head shaved onstage by the band Method of Mayhem, which featured Pamela Anderson's ex, Tommy Lee).

Ozzy and Family in America

Malibu was good to them, but the beachside colony in Los Angeles, where money made the rules, often also made for strange neighbors. It certainly did for Ozzy, Sharon, and the kids.

On one side of their beachside house was Meatloaf, the large singer who'd made his reputation with overblown pop epics before moving on to stage work and films. On the other side, making for an even more spectacular juxtaposition, was Pat Boone, whose fame had come in the fifties by making bland, whitebread versions of black rock'n'roll (which sold incredibly well). He was a Christian—although he had, in fact, tried his own metal album—and a very mainstream person. Not exactly like Ozzy, you might say.

"It was sort of like a Satan sandwich," was the way Sharon would describe the Osbournes and their neighbors.

It probably shouldn't have worked. But curiously, it did. The Osbournes and the Boones got along particularly well, and when Ozzy and his family were on the road, Pat and his wife would look after their house (although you have to wonder what they made of various death heads scattered around the place).

And it was a luxurious place they had, a three-story property right on the beach. Besides Pat Boone and Meatloaf, movie stars like Adam Sandler (who'd become a good friend of Ozzy's) and Shirely MacLaine lived on the same street. Ozzy and Sharon didn't actually own the place, however; they were simply renting while their dream house was being built.

And renting seemed the ideal way to dip the toe into the waters of life in America (and Ozzy insisted that they'd really moved to the U.S. because his children could receive better attention for the Attention Deficit Disorder and dyslexia they suffered—Ozzy too is dyslexic—than they could in England).

Surprisingly, Sharon often didn't feel like they fit in with the Beautiful People who populated Malibu. They had the money— more than many in the area, really—but not quite the grace.

Sharon herself had undergone an operation the year before to lose weight. She'd had a band inserted around her stomach to shrink it. That had helped her go from 224 pounds—which at 5' 2" was a little heavy—to a more manageable, and healthy 129 pounds. And, it had to be said, it helped her fit in physically with the neighborhood.

However, Ozzy wasn't spending all his time lapping up the sun in Malibu. With Ozzfest over, it was time to think about making another record, which would be his first in a long, long time. Back in the fold was guitarist Zakk Wylde, whose work had added a lot to Ozzy's records in the past.

And after years of touring, it really was time for Ozzy to head back to the studio and make a new record. His fans wanted it and he needed it, too, after playing the older material for so long.

But it was also announced that Sabbath would be part of the 2001 Ozzfest, and that their record would finally happen. Having revived the beast, they simply couldn't bear to let it go back to sleep again, or that was the way it seemed. If a record could really happen this time, it would be wonderful. But, of course, rumor had yet to become fact.

Still, it was always unlikely. Ozzy could be full of energy, but even he couldn't work on two records at the same time. And, as much as he loved Sabbath, his own disc had to take priority. It was his name on the line, his focus, and it needed plenty of attention.

He'd had some more medical problems, too. His doctor had sent him to a neurologist, because he thought Ozzy might have Parkinson's disease. It turned out to be a family trait, an hereditary tremor, "but typically my family hadn't bothered mentioning it to me."

Two thousand one started out well, working in the studio and rehearsing both with his own band and Sabbath, but it took a turn for the worse in April. For a break he'd gone back to England and seen his mother. They'd never been in close contact, especially since his father died. However, she was sick now, and he knew this might be his last chance to see her. It was impossible for him not to go, and in the end he was glad he did, because on April 10 she passed away in her sleep at the age of eighty-five.

"Mum died of diabetes and kidney problems. She went peacefully in her sleep, unlike Dad who had cancer and died in pain. I'd been to see her a week before and she seemed fine. I never thought I'd be affected, I wasn't affected when my dad died. But it's different with Mum, it knocks the stuffing out of me. I didn't go to the funeral. They f*** me up too much. I've been to enough funerals to last a lifetime. It might have pushed me over the edge. I thought I was going nuts last year. I was driving around with spears. I was near the dark side. It was like I was waking up with the world's worst hangover but I hadn't had a drink. I'm glued together with medication. I'm on everything, proper psychotic medication. If I don't pop pills I lose it. I'm a f***ing nutter, I won't last to eighty-five."

HOW TO BE AN OZZY PARENT:

Teach your kids to honor their parents by honoring and loving your own.

When his mother died, Ozzy was back in Los Angeles for the ESPN Action and Music Awards show with Sabbath. Perhaps it was good that they were around him at that time. They'd all known each other back in Birmingham, they'd known each other's families, they had a history together. And they were all older, they'd all endured the loss of family members in one form or another. They could all empathize with Ozzy.

The show, like most awards shows, was televised live, and the band was set to close the awards, playing "Paranoid," which had effectively become their signature song over the last three decades.

And they did it before a packed house of stars. Many of the musicians there had toured either with Ozzy himself or as part of Ozzfest (Metallica, members of the Offspring, Linkin Park, the Deftones, NOFX, and Pennywise, for example), while Evel Knieval, Katie Holmes, Darryl Hannah, and skateboarding stars Tony Hawk and Tony Alva were also in attendance.

It was an all-star event, but that was always going to be the way when Sabbath performed. Like the Rolling Stones, or other great bands who'd survived their times and influenced countless others, they'd become legends, an institution. In their case that was all the more so, because there'd been so long when the original quartet hadn't been together.

"It was weird at first," Bill Ward said of the adulation. "Now I'm starting to accept it. I'm totally appreciative of it, and it's an honor . . . It's escalated into a cultish thing. It feels very nice, though."

While he should have been stressed, with so much on his plate, especially the recording of a new album, Ozzy was quite relaxed. He'd even, once again, given up smoking, not the thing most people do when faced with a huge number of time-sensitive tasks. And it was the hardest thing he'd ever had to conquer.

"I've done heroin, coke, LSD, speed, f***ing booze and everything, but that little white cigarette had me nailed down," he said. He'd managed to sometimes sneak a few at home with a reporter, but he hadn't fooled Sharon, who was a nonsmoker. However, this time he finally managed to beat nicotine, which meant he'd effectively given up all his addictions—a huge feat for someone who'd spent so long as an addict to various substances.

OZZY IN QUOTES

"There is something f***ing unbelievable about seeing all of the fans go crazy and chanting 'Ozzy!' I would pay to see them."

"The idea of a band nowadays is five pretty boys, one with a tattoo, one with a shaved head, and on and on. What the f*** is that? I mean, I like Britney Spears, I think she's pretty, but I'm not from the Mickey Mouse Club—I'm from the Godzilla Club!"

"The only black magic Sabbath ever got into was a box of chocolates."

"How can I retire from it? It's not like a job. It's a highly paid hobby."

"Seriously, my only ambition in the world is to go to Egypt, stand on top of the central pyramid, and piss all over it."

"F*** off! I'm not taking the blame for that crap!" (on eighties pop music)

"I think we should train monkeys to smoke and drink, cuz, you know, smoking and drinking monkeys would be funny."

"After I bit the head off the bat, the animal rights people came after me every night. Probably right after they finished eating their Colonel Sanders or whatever, telling me I shouldn't be biting the heads off bats. I'll tell you what bats taste like. Like a good McDonald's."

"My mother was an amateur singer, my father was an amateur drunk."

"I'll never be mellow. I'd sooner die than become a boring old fart. I'm still as much of a loon as I ever was. I like being a little crazy—it makes people respect you. They never take you for granted, that's for sure."

"Why would I ever consider giving up what I'm doing? I love doing it, and the fans seem to love it as much as I do. If I wasn't doing this, I'd end up either in prison or at the end of a rope in a very short time. I don't even like to consider the possibility."

HOW TO BE AN OZZY PARENT:

Give up all your bad habits; that way your kids will be less tempted.

By the time Ozzfest 2001 got under way, Ozzy was a complete nonsmoker. But if anything could have caused a relapse, it was the sheer size of the movable feast. Twenty-four bands, with Ozzy doing double duty every night, performing both with his own group and as Sabbath's singer. For the first time in several years, he had new material to try on the audiences, and they just ate it up.

Sharon's acute instinct for music had helped her put together the kind of bill to make any metal fan drool. In addition to the two headliners, there was Marilyn Manson, Slipknot, Linkin Park, and Papa Roach, any of whom could have headlined their own tours. It was, essentially, the tour to end all tours, and fans responded to the artists, coming in record numbers to see them perform. Followed by a CD, *Ozzfest: The Second Millennium,* it continued to be the kind of success Lollapalooza and Lilith Fair had hoped to be, but had never achieved in any kind of long run. While alternative had become mainstream (or simply withered away), the audience for metal had been established ever since Sabbath burst on the scene, and it wasn't going away. It never would. At the same time, Ozzy was baffled by the way it kept going.

"I keep saying to Sharon, 'How long is it gonna go?' And she'll go, 'We'll know when it's time to pull out.' Every year it gets bigger and bigger, what else am I gonna do?"

But he was back with a vengeance. On August 25, his new single, "Gets Me Through" aired on the radio for the first time, and *Down to Earth,* a brand-new album, finally appeared in stores on October 16. For the cover, Ozzy spent half a day being X-rayed, with some very interesting results.

By the time the album came out, however, the world had changed. September 11 had come and gone, and what everyone knew was upside down. Ozzy had been in New York when it all happened. His assistant had called him, and told him to switch on the television, that a plane had just hit the Twin Towers. Then the other plane hit, and "I'm screaming, 'Sharon, for f***'s sake, f***ing watch this shit!' When they both collapsed, f***, I couldn't believe it, man."

His instinct was to get back to his children, all the way across the country in California. But the airports were closed, so flying wasn't an option—even if he could have gotten on a plane then, anyway.

But being a star with clout could pay some dividends. He called his tour manager, who managed to locate a bus. However, it was in Nashville. It was driven to New York, arriving just as the tunnels were reopened.

"We got on the bus and just as we got out of New York, they closed the f***ing tunnel again. It was unbelievable. It was a stroke of f***ing luck to get out."

But get out, and back to California they did, to be reunited with Aimee, Kelly, and Jack. It was just a short respite, though, as Ozzy was due to hit the road—beginning on Halloween, naturally—with his Night of Merry Mayhem tour, supported by Rob Zombie, Mudvayne, Soil, and OneSideZero.

Disaster of a sort struck even before the first note, though. Ozzy slipped in the shower of his Tucson hotel room before the opening show. He suffered a stress fracture in his leg, although he didn't realize it at the time. He continued playing every night, the pain worsening each day, until he finally had to go to the doctor on November 8. The diagnosis was simple, and so was the cure. He had to stay off his leg until it had healed—which meant that a number of dates had to be postponed.

It would be late November before he was able to get back on the road, just after Rob Zombie had directed Ozzy's video for "Dreamer," the ballad off *Down to Earth*. Although it seemed as if it fit the times, it hadn't been written about 9/11; the sentiments just happened to be perfectly suited for it.

And, in fact, Ozzy would perform a benefit for the victims of the World Trade Center disaster on December 23, at the Meadowlands in New Jersey. The proceeds went to the Howard Stern 9/11 fund, as the shock jock was an old friend of Ozzy's. He also visited Ground Zero, and was given a cross made of iron from the wreckage, presented by New York police and firemen.

The tragedy had affected him deeply, as it did everyone in America, and throughout the world.

But life had to go on, and so did music, which could be a healer. Ozzy had a tour planned for February, going back to Japan, where he wanted to make a live album at the famed Budokan venue. But that was just the first stop on what was going to be one of his longest jaunts ever. He'd also be hitting Korea (where he'd be performing a USO show for the troops, and would get to drive a tank), making his first-ever stop in Alaska, then going through Canada, before flying to Germany.

And 2002 was going to be Ozzy's best year ever. In March *The Osbournes* premiered on MTV. Ozzy and Sharon had been featured on the channel before, in 2001, when the *Cribs* series ran and featured their house.

They'd been almost a staple of VH1, too. As part of its *Behind the Music* series, they'd covered Ozzy's career—and that had included interviews with Sharon, both as his wife and manager. One of the most popular episodes, perhaps because of its humor and outrage, had aired an incredible sixty-five times.

TV loved Ozzy. He was naturally funny and deadpan, and not afraid to poke fun at himself. All his years onstage had made him into a remarkable entertainer, and Ozzfest had largely made his name into a franchise. Since the first one, in 1996, his profile had just continued to rise. He was, essentially, the pleasant face of heavy metal in America.

HOW TO BE AN OZZY PARENT:

Everyone has a talent. Teach your kids to make the most of what they've got.

He'd gone beyond scary to become something that was more Teddy bear than heavy metal monster. The Prince of Darkness was just as appealing in the light.

How far he'd come became apparent in April, when, in front of an audience including Marilyn Manson and Robbin Williams, he got his star on the Hollywood Walk of Fame on Hollywood Boulevard. Maybe it wasn't that big a deal—lots of people had them—but it was a sign of even greater acceptance by the establishment.

But nothing was greater acceptance than being a guest at the White House. That happened in early May, when Ozzy and Sharon were the guests of a journalist at a correspondents' dinner. President Bush, who, according to some reports was a fan of *The*

Osbournes, addressed the crowd, and knew full well that Ozzy was in attendance. Which was why he said, "The thing about Ozzy is, he's made a lot of big hit recordings—'Party with the Animals,' 'Sabbath Bloody Sabbath,' 'Face in Hell,' 'Black Skies,' and 'Bloodbath in Paradise.' Ozzy, your mom loves your stuff."

Did he ask for Ozzfest tickets, though—either for himself or his daughters? No one was saying, but it's a fair bet that he wouldn't be refused, with VIP all-access privileges. Although his daughters might be banned from the beer garden.

But there was plenty happening during the evening in Washington. Ozzy was the one thronged by journalists, not the president, and when one asked what he might request from Bush, Ozzy replied, "Dual citizenship. I want to be American. America is the coolest place on the face of the earth. You've got freedom of speech. You've got McDonald's."

But perhaps the best comment of the night (besides Ozzy telling the president that he needed to wear his hair a little longer), came from comedian Drew Carey, who pointed out: "First of all, they both love their families. They both partied a little too hard when they were younger. Half the time you can't understand a word either one of them is saying. And neither one of them can make a move without their wife's approval."

And when the dinner was over? It was Ozzy who was signing autographs for politicians—for their families, of course—and being mobbed once again by reporters.

But then it was back to work again for Sharon and Ozzy, getting busy on Ozzfest, which was going ahead once more, in its seventh incarnation. It had taken on a complete life of its own. With twenty-one bands in all, it just kept growing; in addition to Ozzy himself, there were plenty of big names on the main stage, including System of a Down, P.O.D., and Rob Zombie. With thirty-one dates spread over two months, it was also the biggest and most adventurous tour to date, as if the festival was really spreading its wings. And it was certainly showing no signs of a downturn in popularity.

How big can Ozzy get? Well, right now the sky appeared to be the limit. Not only was he in demand from the White House, but also from the world's most famous secret agent. For his new movie, *Austin Powers in Goldmember,* comedian/actor Mike Myers planned on finishing his filming at Ozzy and Sharon's Beverly Hills home.

Everything was coming up Ozzy. Even his old albums were being reissued—but with a twist. *Blizzard of Ozz, Diary of a Madman, Tribute,* and *No More Tears* were coming out in remastered versions, with new liner notes, and, in the case of the first two, re-recorded bass and drums erasing the original tracks by Daisley and Kerslake. It was Ozzy's decision, Sharon said.

Add to that the fact that he was in the process of recording some new tracks for his *Live at Budokan* release, and he continued to be a busy man. The only downside had come with the death, from cancer, of former drummer Randy Castillo.

Even his offspring were becoming involved in music. Kelly was recording with two members of Incubus, and Jack was continuing to help Sharon scout bands for both Ozzfest and the Epic record label. And Ozzy's son from his first marriage, Louis, was making a name for himself as a techno DJ, spinning around Britain and Europe, even in the clubbing hot spot of Ibiza, and venturing as far as the U.S.

HOW TO BE AN OZZY PARENT:

Be proud of your kids when they succeed.

At fifty-three, Ozzy was more popular than ever before. He'd graduated from music to being a celebrity, was a regular guest on Jay Leno's talk show—in fact various members of the family had been on most of the chat shows. Ozzy and Sharon had been guests at the New York Stock Exchange (of course, having $58 million will get you invited places). From being very much on the outside, Ozzy had become a pillar of the establishment. He'd even donated money to People for the Ethical Treatment of Animals to help stop cruelty in Korea, one of the countries where the World Cup 2002 was to be staged.

Of course, Ozzy really is an animal lover himself. For all his history, he likes pets, especially his dogs, and the three cats who coexist with them. But it all goes to prove that he's put the outrageous past behind him. He's established himself as Ozzy. Everyone's heard the rumors about him, the stories and tales of his history—he's a legend, and not only in rock circles—for his consumption and excesses.

But, above all, he's a good father, as *The Osbournes* has proved. He might not do it in the most conventional way, but he truly loves his family—he's devoted to them. He relies on Sharon in a way most husbands never could, to the extent of saying, and meaning, "We have a pact. She's not allowed to die before me. I couldn't live without her."

To many, the Osbournes might seem like a dysfunctional family. After all, isn't that what you'd expect from a rich musician and his wife and kids? And they may not be the norm for American suburbia. But Beverly Hills has never tried to be suburbia, and Ozzy and Sharon aren't even American, let alone the traditional suburban types.

At the core is the relationship Ozzy and Sharon share. With divorce rates so high, especially in the music business, for a couple to stay married for twenty years says a great deal. That's doubly true when they share business and a home life. And it certainly hasn't been smooth sailing; it's weathered Ozzy's alcoholism and drug addiction, his groupies, and the fact that he's been gone on tour as much as he's been at home. It's even overcome him trying to strangle his wife, the kind of barrier that would leave most marriages virtually dead in the water.

So what exactly is their bond? What's the magic that keeps them together? To say it's love would be a simple answer, but obviously true. They care very, very deeply about each other, and have for many years. And they share their children. Sharon's a strong woman, and her strength is a rock for Ozzy, who's proved in the past that he's someone who can easily succumb to temptation. He relies on her for a lot of things, not only in his business, but also in everyday life. She wears the pants in the family, and that's fine with him. She puts desperately needed order into his life.

They've shared a great deal over the years. No one knows Ozzy as well as Sharon, and vice versa. In the early days they could be as wild as each other, but with motherhood and the pressures of running a business, Sharon was forced to tone a lot of that down.

WHO SAID...?

1. "One thing I didn't realize was that my parents had the first Black Sabbath album in their collection."

2. "I enrolled my kids in a Christian school in L.A."

3. "We've never had a safety net. We've always been like, Oh, s***. If this doesn't work, we're in the toilet."

4. (After being asked, "What was your worst nightmare?") "When Ozzy was in the band—oops—sorry, joking about."

5. "Okay, Ozzy . . . Might have been a mistake."

6. "You know, I used to listen to heavy metal: Slayer, Judas Priest, Ozzy, then a Michael Bolton marathon came on so I smashed my stereo!!"

7. "Were not going to have freakin' Judas Priest play here, that could steal away my band!!"

8. "After Ozzy heard what had happened I had to go to the hospital to have his foot taken out of my a**."

9. *"Make no mistake, the eleven tracks inside rock. In places it could be any Ozzy/Black Sabbath album from 1970."*

10. *"I like celebrating, whether it's in Beverly Hills or f***ing Timbuktu!"*

11. *"I hate Christmas. I just think that it's a big windup to get money out of people. I'm not Scrooge, I just think that it's for kids, not for me."*

12. *"You know, I do have one ambition left in life. I want to see my grandchildren. I just want to see my kids go through the s*** that I went through with them!"*

13. *"She says her real father is a builder or something."*

There were too many things going on in life for her not to be focused. So perhaps she let that side loose vicariously through Ozzy. To be fair, she did try to restrain him in some areas—getting him into rehab, for example—but she enjoyed others. And any publicity was good publicity for someone playing metal music; the fans ate it all up.

Of course, with provocation Sharon could unleash her wild side—anyone who'd throw an entire ham over the fence because the neighbors were playing their music too loud (which is a defi-

OZZY QUIZ: ANSWERS

1. *Marilyn Manson*

2. *Ozzy*

3. *Sharon*

4. *Tony Iommi*

5. *George W. Bush*

6. *Wrestler "Stone Cold" Steve Austin*

7. *Ozzy*

8. *Sharon*

9. *Ozzy*

10. *Ozzy*

11. *Ozzy*

12. *Ozzy*

13. *Sharon, on oldest daughter Aimee*

nite irony in itself, but the Osbournes try to be good neighbors. When classical guitarist Leona Boyd, who lives across the street, complained about Jack playing his drums in the garage, he stopped.) can obviously have her moments over the top.

She's fiercely protective of Ozzy—well, of all her family—in a way most wives aren't. But then, most husbands aren't as vulnerable as Ozzy. The years of abuse have taken their toll on him, but that's perhaps inevitable. And she looks after him. She's social in a way he isn't (this is, after all, a man who said he'd like to spend "a year at home with a big box of popcorn, watching TV and drinking Diet Pepsis"), always happy to press the flesh, see new people. She keeps him from withdrawing into himself, and she makes sure he stays active, busy, and occupied. She gives Ozzy a space where he can turn off as a performer and simply relax as himself, and that's the kind of cushion he's always needed, to be able to leave the road behind him, a cocoon where he can escape and unwind—which, these days, often means just watching the History Channel.

And things have doubtless been easier since Ozzy quit alcohol and illegal drugs. There's little danger now of him running off in women's clothing and urinating on the Alamo (although he still seems a little hazy on what always constitutes a toilet). And, for all that it's part of the mythology, it's twenty years since he's bitten the head off anything.

Sharon's his calming influence, in general, although she's quite capable of getting worked up about things, and neither of them moderates their language at home—but Sharon does seem to know when "f***" isn't an appropriate word.

In a world that too rarely acknowledges such a thing, they're soul mates, two sides of the same coin who are a complete complement to each other. Together they make a whole, and that's a wonderful thing.

On her side, Sharon adores Ozzy. He's never been just a client. She fought to become his manager, she's taken him back even after he tried to kill her, and she's watched out for him, guided his career, and been his guardian angel.

She can swear at him, laugh at him, but she always loves him. She is, perhaps, the only one he'll really listen to. He trusts her implicitly, which is something he hasn't been able to say about many people in his life. She's always been in his corner, no matter what the battle, and always will be. It's a beautiful thing.

HOW TO BE AN OZZY PARENT:

If you can't be with the one you love, don't love the one you're with.

Osbournes, Meet the Osbournes . . .

The Osbournes didn't just materialize out of thin air to become the biggest show ever aired on MTV in its twenty-one-year history or the most popular show on cable. Like any good baby, it had a long gestation period.

It all began several years ago with a *Behind the Music* documentary about Ozzy on VH-1, the more adult sister of MTV. His tales of madness and mayhem—and his deadpan, funny way of telling a story—became incredibly popular; the episode ended up being shown sixty-five times.

It might all have been left at that, except for Ozzy's resurgence in popularity, thanks to Ozzfest. Suddenly he was an important musical figure again, and MTV approached him and Sharon for an episode of their show, *Cribs*. The idea was to peek behind the scenes and see the way musicians and their families really lived away from the limelight.

At that point, the Osbournes were in their Malibu house, with Pat Boone on one side, and Meatloaf on the other. While not exactly "their" house—it was a rental—they'd made it into their own, with Sharon's beloved magazines around, Ozzy's Beatles books, the small horde of dogs and cats, and the trappings of everyday life in America; computers, satellite television, and three children.

What the cameras picked up, while filming during the year 2000, was the remarkable bond the family shared, and their incredible humor. Without meaning to be, Ozzy was a comedian of great talent, so deadpan that you never knew if he was serious. It was enough to intrigue executives at MTV.

But, according to some sources, they weren't the only ones. According to a story released in January 2001 by Ananova, a company called Threshold Entertainment was making an Internet sitcom called *Ozzy and Harriet,* a spoof of the 1950s television show of that name, starring Ozzy and Sharon. It would be set in Beverly Hills, and star Ozzy as, well, Ozzy.

"His personal lifestyle is so engaging and enduring—and as funny as h***," said Threshold chairman Larry Kasanoff.

It was an interesting idea. But obviously, it never happened, perhaps because of the massive downturn in tech stocks that occurred in March 2001, forcing those Internet companies that didn't go bust to lower their expectations.

There was talk about transferring the sitcom idea to television, and even discussions regarding the idea. But once more, nothing happened.

It was actually Jack who came up with the concept for *The Osbournes,* although he was thinking on a much smaller scale than a ten-week series. His idea was for a crew to spend a weekend at the house: "It'd be like *The Real World* but with us."

But that still didn't mean it would automatically happen. Sharon was in discussions with MTV, and they were exploring plenty of options. She and Ozzy had stories to tell, and the network loved what they were hearing.

Reality shows were big in 2001—*Survivor, Temptation Island,* and others. But there'd never been a show that just followed a family around, unscripted. However, there could be a market for one. That was why, when Sharon mentioned Jack's idea to the network, they became very, very interested.

Of course, there was still a lot to be ironed out. To begin with, there were the logistics of having a camera crew around. How long would it last, what would be filmed, what wouldn't?

The process became easier when Sharon announced that they were getting ready to move into their new house, going from Malibu to the place in Beverly Hills, just off Sunset Boulevard.

It was a spacious place—as well it should have been with a price tag of $4.5 million. With a wall and sturdy gates, it offered plenty of privacy, a standard for the houses of stars.

The property included a pool house and a large garage. There were, however, enough guest bedrooms for the production crew to be able to take over two of them as offices, and mount twelve cameras around the house to film unobtrusively for eighteen hours a day, every day except Sunday.

Everything was in place by the time the family moved into the house in October. The crew was committed to being as out of sight as possible, even if it meant climbing in and out of one of the office windows to stay out of the way.

"We could have gone through the garage," explained Greg

Johnston, who was the show's executive producer. "But we wanted to make sure we didn't p*** them off. At any point if they wanted to kick us out, they could have."

Not that it was likely to happen. Having agreed to the deal, Ozzy and Sharon weren't about to back out. It was great publicity, both for Ozzy and for Ozzfest, and it was likely to make cult stars out of the entire family.

All except Aimee, that is. She'd always gone her own way, and was beginning a singing career. She wanted to do that on her own, without the push of the show. She was still very much a part of the Osbourne family, even if she did think her parents were "geeks," and often insisted that Ozzy couldn't be her real father. She loved her parents and her siblings, but she was tired of all the bat taunts she'd had at school and elsewhere. She was adult enough to want to make it on her own. And so, for the duration of the filming, which was scheduled to last four months, she moved into a guest house on the property, not to be seen on camera.

HOW TO BE AN OZZY PARENT:

Sometimes it's best to let your kids make their own decisions.

However much the film crews tried to fade into the background, with three crews around, it was impossible. They were simply *there*, and everyone had to accept that, which they seemed to do with plenty of grace. And everyone had to hold their breath, and hope the footage would be good enough to use.

"We had really no idea what we were going to get," said Brian Graden, president of MTV Entertainment. "We simply started collecting footage. . . . We began to see that a lot of these story lines mirrored classic domestic sitcom story lines, yet with a twist of outrageousness that you wouldn't believe."

One thing that did remain sacred was Sunday. The crews could be there six days a week, filming everything that went on over an eighteen-hour period, but on Sunday the family would be left alone.

Something that quickly became apparent was that the Osbournes might have money and status, but they were very much a family, caring for and about each other. And the problems they had were things almost every family with teenage kids could relate to.

"We have the same problems as anybody else," Sharon pointed out. "It's all relative, whether you're in the public eye or not, whether you have money or don't. You still have to deal with your kids and the issues of smoking pot and doing homework."

HOW TO BE AN OZZY PARENT:

Make sure your kids do their chores.

But they did their parenting with plenty of their own particular style. Never having had to look at themselves, seeing the daily

THE OSBOURNES QUIZ

1. How many film crews did MTV use?

2. And how many cameras did they have?

3. What were the cameras wired into?

4. How did they get in and out of the house?

5. Which family member didn't want to be part of the show?

6. Where did she live instead?

7. Which family member will be recording "Papa Don't Preach" for the series soundtrack CD?

8. And with musicians from what band?

9. Who will be producing the CD?

10. How many dogs do the Osbournes have?

11. Where do the Osbournes live?

12. How much did the house cost?

13. How many stoves does the house have?

14. Does the house have cable or satellite TV?

15. What kind of car does Sharon drive?

OZZY QUIZ: ANSWERS

1. Three

2. Twelve

3. The house security system

4. Through a bedroom window

5. Aimee

6. In a guest house on the grounds

7. Kelly

8. Incubus

9. Jack

10. Seven

11. Beverly Hills, just off Sunset Boulevard

12. $4.5 million

13. Four

14. Satellite

15. Mercedes

footage was an illuminating experience for every single one of them. Still, part of the deal was that nothing be left out, although swear words were bleeped—and there were plenty of them.

"We're not the Partridge family," Sharon said. "It had to be real or we wouldn't do it. MTV agreed to do it as it was and just leave it pure. We all learned a lot about ourselves—that we all swear too much and have bad tempers."

Whether pure was the appropriate word was debatable, but it worked. And what the people at MTV saw was that they had more than just a fly-on-the-wall reality show about the family life of metal's biggest hero—they had the world's first reality sitcom. Without even trying, Ozzy was hilarious, and there was definitely something bizarre, for example, in seeing a man idolized by millions taking out the garbage. To Ozzy, it made no sense.

"I don't bloody understand why people think it's funny, me taking out the trash. I mean, I'm a guy. I don't have a f***ing trash roadie."

And really, Ozzy had no idea if there was anything worthwhile in what they were filming, until the first cut of the first episode appeared at the house. He asked the film crew—the people who'd essentially been living with them for weeks, to view it.

"I said, 'You all work for me, but be totally honest. Tell me what you really think. It's me being me in my house. I don't have a script.' When I came in later, they were all cracking up laughing."

A great deal of the pleasure was the fact that it was totally unscripted and perfectly natural—a family interacting as they always had and always would. And there was a certain surreal charm in watching boxes marked LINENS, DEVIL HEADS, and DEAD THINGS being unpacked. It was life in the raw—well, as raw as it could get in

Beverly Hills, in a mansion tailored to the Osbourne tastes, with a massive kitchen that held four stoves, and a huge billiard room.

Calling it palatial hardly did it justice. And the family's dogs certainly loved it, given the run of the house, yard, and even the pool. The only problem with that was that they weren't properly housebroken, which meant everyone had to watch where they walked.

Still, they were used to it (even if the film crews weren't). Moreover, they were getting paid for it. At a reported $20,000 per episode, it wasn't a spectacular payday by Ozzy standards, but the potential long-term rewards were much greater. It would bring Ozzy into the homes of the precious MTV demographic—the people aged fifteen and up, all the way to thirty-four.

And that could bring them out to his shows, and get them buying his records. While Ozzfest attracted a very diverse age range, Ozzy's own crowd was getting decidedly older, in the boomer range. And that meant they had interests and responsibilities that extended beyond music and buying CDs.

With the television series, Ozzy could become the dad every kid wished he or she had. His history and his involvement with music made him incredibly cool—who wouldn't want the godfather of metal for a father? That's not to say it was solely a calculated move on Sharon's part, purely to gain Ozzy a new audience. But seeing him in his home environment would help soften those historical edges which had made him such a beast to the Christian right, and show he really was a gentle family man.

After all, he'd announced, after he quit drinking, that "I'm putting 'Ozzy' on the shelf . . . I created a monster, you know? People think I walk around the f***ing street like that."

But living down the bat and the dove had been largely impossible. More than the music, more than Sabbath even, those were the things everyone remembered. And if the show could change that perception, it would be doing something worthwhile.

After all, Ozzy was fifty-three now. His years of outrage were long behind him. These days, in the main, he was an upright citizen (although he did have a problem with the painkiller Vicodin, following the stress fracture in his leg in late 2001). He'd become . . . cuddly. And it was time to show the world that the Ozzy they thought they knew was quite different, and very lovable.

But, as someone at MTV said, "No one could write the characters of Ozzy, Sharon, Jack, and Kelly; they're simply too real."

Still, too real was what was expected, even if the network then discovered they were having to bleep almost every sentence that was spoken. But, if you wanted the Osbournes, that was what you got. They weren't about to censor themselves, as Sharon pointed out. Now *that* wouldn't be natural.

"We could have gone 'Good morning, daaaling. How was your day?' Ozzy laughed. "That would have been like f***upsville. With our family, you take the good with the bad."

The one thing that always was evident—indeed, it couldn't be hidden—was the love in the family. By some standards they were hardly normal, but what did that matter? At the heart, they showed more love than most families. And as Ozzy noted, "What is a functional family? I know I'm dysfunctional by a long shot, but what guidelines do we all have to go by? The Waltons?"

MTV certainly didn't have high hopes for the series. If it managed the same kind of ratings as most shows on the channel, it would attract about half a million viewers. While that would have been good, it wasn't about to break any records. But they'd have been satisfied with that. After all, it was Ozzy, not the usual subject matter for the channel and its younger audience. But they also knew the show was funny, and a couple of months before it was due to start airing, they held a press conference—with the family in attendance—to show it to journalists.

Perhaps surprisingly, the press did turn out in force, although they didn't seem to know what to expect, but were pleasantly surprised, if a little baffled. One reporter asked if MTV might close-caption the show, given Ozzy's thick Midlands accent. The question didn't sit too well with Sharon, who made the reporter stand up before caustically replying, "That's my husband!" (A few years before, MTV had been forced to offer a translation of an interview with the English band Oasis, because their thick accents made the words largely unintelligible to an American audience.)

Ozzy was a bit more diplomatic, saying that "If the people can't understand what the f*** I'm saying, they'll send in letters to MTV and then they'll subtitle it."

However, what they saw obviously left a warm and fuzzy impression with reviewers, although, in *Entertainment Weekly*, Ken Tucker did wonder, "Are we laughing with Ozzy or at him, and does this distinction even matter to the MTV audience?" But he left very positive about the family values of the show, as did others.

In *Time*, James Poniewozik wrote: "The Osbournes are the oldest thing on TV since the test pattern: a nuclear family that eats meals together, shares its problems . . . and survives wacky scenarios. But," he added, "the pace is leisurely, not forced, and the

OSBOURNE HOUSE FACTOIDS

1. There's a painting of Sodom and Gomorrah in the foyer.

2. The family's seven dogs are named Maggie, New Baby, Minnie, Martin, Pipi (actually Aimee's dog, who was lost, and then found in Apple Valley), Lulu, and Lola (the part-time pet).

3. The billiards room has stained-glass doors salvaged from church windows in Los Angeles.

4. The toilet in Ozzy's movie theater room is actually a urinal—because he always pees on the seat.

5. The ceiling in the dining room is painted to look like a blue sky with clouds.

6. Kelly has a collection of chairs from the sixties and seventies in her room, including one from the set of A Clockwork Orange.

7. Jack collects toothbrushes, and has a studded leather bed.

humor derives less from 'jokes' than from characters who . . . surprise you."

The bottom line was that Ozzy and the family were simply being the way they were every single day. This was them, this was their routine.

"People go, 'Oh, that's so funny, Ozzy, when you run up the stairs' and the dog craps on my carpet, you know. It's normal for me . . . We just went with what is normal."

How many fathers could turn around and tell their families—"I love you all. I love you all more than life itself, but you're all f***ing mad." Now that's real, unadulterated love.

HOW TO BE AN OZZY PARENT:

Tell your family that you love them—often.

But a family that can be so open, can love openly, too. It was evident in the frequent hugs and kisses Ozzy and Sharon would give each other, much to the embarrassment of Kelly, who thought of her parents as too old to be doing that kind of thing.

Still, Ozzy would cuddle and hug his daughter, too. And she never minded that. It was reassuring to come across someone who felt comfortable enough with himself—or possibly uninhibited enough—to still be able to do that, without even thinking about it.

For all that Ozzy could seem to not be completely there, often tuning out conversations—included those aimed directly at him—

he remained very much aware of what was going on all around in the house. He could happily bury himself in the History Channel for hours at a time—this was, after all, a man whose ambition was to spend a year watching television—but he still seemed acutely tuned in to vibrations within the family. Of course, he couldn't always hear was what being said to him. As he pointed out to Kelly: if she'd spent the last thirty years standing in front of excess decibels, her hearing probably wouldn't be too great, either.

Possibly the best, and in some ways the healthiest, thing about the Osbournes was their lack of repression. They could fight and make up, swear and vent, and still be a happy family. It was the way everyone should be, but few really were. Counselors and psychologists would have to agree that in some respects, at least, they were an ideal family.

Of course, you can take not being repressed a bit too far—such as Sharon's ham-throwing incident, when she admitted, "At the end I thought I was quite insane." She'd unraveled a bit too far then. But it made for great television. And it was real—how many people had fantasized about doing something similar to thoughtless neighbors, but would never have dared?

But that mix of the bizarre and the mundane was exactly what made *The Osbournes* so wonderful. You never knew exactly where it might turn next. Each episode had a structure of sorts, albeit fairly loose, with some kind of resolution at the end—after all, it was a reality sitcom, which meant it needed a beginning and end, but in the middle it could be as bizarre as anything off *Monty Python's Flying Circus*.

And it was a peek into the way the other half lives, which turned out to be no different—except for the money and the larger house—than most other people. The basic problems remain exactly the same. How do you work the remote? Ask the kids. And then follow that up with some father-son bonding over a program or two.

In many ways Ozzy's a big kid himself. It's a legacy of the rock- 'n'roll lifestyle, perhaps, of being looked after, and having every whim served for so long. That isn't to say he's lacking in responsi- bility, by any means. He can be a very traditional parent of the do- as-I-say, not-as-I-do variety. The difference is, he's earned the right to be that way.

Very few (if any) fathers have done what Ozzy's done, gone to his extremes and come back again. He's done almost everything, all kinds of drugs and drink, had women offer themselves to him more times than he can count. That's rock'n'roll, especially on the level of a major star. And he doesn't dole out advice to his children lightly. He does it bluntly.

"I ain't got time for all that soft soap stuff," he admitted. So when he sat his girls down he simply said, "If you're going to have a d*** pushed in you, make sure he wears a condom. That's sensi- ble advice, isn't it?" And he was just as forthright with his son.

And when Ozzy tells his kids not to drink or do drugs, there's years of experience behind the words. Anyone who's been in rehab fourteen times has the knowledge—but this papa doesn't preach.

Well, not usually. When Kelly got a tattoo—a little heart way up high on her left hip—Ozzy did preach a little, telling her about the infection he once suffered from a tattoo (and Ozzy, after all, has arms full of the things). It was a warning. But he also knew he had to tell Sharon what their daughter had done, calling her during a hair appointment, even though Kelly begged him not to. The Osbourne parents have no secrets from each other—and how many couples can honestly say *that*?

One thing no one in the family knew was how well the show would be received, or what kind of an audience they'd find in television land. At one point during the filming, Jack said, "Dad, I'm not ready for this." Ozzy replied, "It's too late."

And it was. The network was still deciding how many episodes to air. Originally eight had been announced, then people said it could go up to thirteen. The final figure, as all fans know well, was ten. Ozzy himself didn't even want to watch it, because, he said, "I don't like to see myself in the real world on TV talking. I have a singing voice. And I have . . . a voice now. And when I see myself like this on TV, I go, I don't like to see myself straight on TV."

So when the show did begin to air, in March, he was relatively oblivious to it being shown—of course, he'd also been focusing on the end of his recent tour. None of it hit him until he was out in Los Angeles.

"I was walking down the street last Saturday and people that normally wouldn't stop me are freaking out with this. I had just come off tour in Canada, so I was kind of blind to the response. I got back on Friday and suddenly people are stopping me on the street and screaming at me. In fact an ambulance goes past me and the guy goes, 'Hey Ozzy, Hello, yeah'—on the intercom there. 'Good show, man you gotta keep it up . . . ' I'm kind of flipping out, you know?"

Think about it—how many people would feel comfortable with their lives up on screen? Even if almost every third word was bleeped, it was in the raw, and there for all to see. People in music live their lives in a fishbowl—although it had been many years since Ozzy had been fodder for the tabloids. These days he lived the quiet life of no outrage, simply doing his job as a singer and entertainer when he wasn't at home.

He could also be every bit as silly as his kids at times, especially when they were younger, and he was still drinking.

"I remember one time when I was drunk at our last house in L.A. . . . on Christmas Eve. I was shaking these bells outside their window, yelling out 'I can hear Father Christmas coming!' Meanwhile, I'm falling all about the garden with these silly sleigh bells. My kids had to get up out of bed to go tell my wife, 'Tell Daddy to come in and go to bed, because we can't sleep with all the noise he's making.' "

But closeness had been hard-won. For the first several years of their lives, Ozzy had drunk heavily. They'd gone on tour with him at times, more so when they were older. They'd grown up in the music business, which was one reason Jack often went to clubs, with and without his mother, helping to scout new talent—a better reason than most boys his age. Along with Kelly, Jack was quite capable of dishing the dirt on celebrities—whether the camera was running or not—and pushing at the boundaries with his parents, as all teenagers will.

Still, considering their unusual upbringing, the kids were both very normal. As one psychologist noted, they were well-adjusted, because their parents actually let them talk, and listened to what they had to say, even if they didn't always agree with it. But the Osbourne household was one of self-expression, largely held together by Sharon and the Australian nanny/au pair/assistant Melinda, who was capable of handling any crisis and keeping everyone in line.

HOW TO BE AN OZZY PARENT:

Don't be afraid of letting your kids express their opinions. Loudly, if they need to.

For all the Englishness of Ozzy and Sharon, it was a very California lifestyle, with its pool and home theater, and pet therapists for the dogs—much to Ozzy's disgust.

Once home, Ozzy wasn't one for socializing much; he was happier with the peace and quiet. But even then, every day would be filled. He'd dress in a T-shirt and one of his forty pairs of black track pants, work out, go and see his therapist, then rehearse or be involved in promotion, recording, or whatever else needed to be done. By his own admission, Ozzy really didn't have much idea about dressing himself. Usually, if they were going somewhere special, Sharon would select his clothes; whenever he tried, she'd end up saying, "Are you f***ing joking, you're going to walk down the street like that?" But it was certainly better than putting on one of her dresses and walking around in public. . . .

Where Ozzy could easily relax, Sharon was the complete opposite, an "absolute complete lunatic workaholic," as Ozzy called her. With so much on her plate—managing Ozzy, looking after Ozzfest, and other things—she needed to be. And unlike him, she only got four to five hours of sleep a night, often out late catching bands in the clubs, then up early to make her phone calls to Europe, which was eight or nine hours ahead of California. She lived with a phone glued to her ear. But she was also responsible for the kids, getting them up and out, ready for school, and handling plenty of the chores around the house—a Supermom, really, but just like many other working mothers who had to juggle parenting and work.

For all that she'd get out and around to clubs, Kelly didn't care for L.A. that much. She'd liked it when she was younger, around twelve or thirteen, but now she saw through the superficiality of it all, and had discovered that "when you get older the actual people that are here just seem so unhappy all the time. Everyone's so skinny with fake tits and blond hair. I kind of don't fit into that here."

Like his sister, Jack enjoyed hanging out, and he had the time for it, just being home-schooled for three hours a day (and not getting up until 9 A.M.—probably just as well, given his tendency to keep late hours). After that it was on to his job at Epic Records, where he was employed scouting new bands (one of his recommendations had reached a development deal, but had yet to be formally signed). He was as cynical about Los Angeles and the cult of celebrity as Kelly, noting that "if I was just a regular kid, half the people wouldn't even come up and acknowledge my existence."

But he wasn't a regular kid. He was the son of a star, and about to become a star in his own right, as the series began airing. The same would be true of Kelly—and Sharon would be a much more recognizable figure than she'd ever been. But that was the price you paid for being on television in America.

No one, not even the most optimistic network executive, could have predicted the way the show took off. Perhaps it was the articles in newspapers around the country that intrigued people. Or perhaps people were simply curious as to what Ozzy's home life might be about. Maybe people needed to laugh after the months of sadness following September 11. Whatever the reason, it started out more strongly than they'd expected, even if it wasn't yet quite a blockbuster. It was repeated a few times during the week, with equally good results (reruns generally don't perform as well as the original airing).

The second week brought a big increase in viewers, mostly through word of mouth as those who'd seen the first episode told their friends. And the figures continued to climb. It was a little at a time to begin with, then a spike that put it through the roof by the fourth week. MTV had a hit on its hands. It was ironic that it came from heavy metal, the style the channel had long ago abandoned in favor of hip-hop and more teen-oriented material.

This outdid anything they'd had before. There were five million viewers. The week after it was six. That made it, beyond any shadow of a doubt, the most popular show MTV had shown since it went on the air in 1981. And it wasn't a spike that slipped away again. The viewing figures brought more publicity, and that brought more viewers, curious to see the phenomenon. From being MTV's biggest show, suddenly it was the most popular show on cable, and showing up high in the Nielsen ratings.

Who'd have thought it?

Suddenly, the Osbourne house wasn't quite the private property it had been. The Hollywood tour buses started driving by, twenty of them every day, giving out-of-towners the tours of the stars' homes. And people would simply show up and wait outside the gates, hoping one member of the family or another would drive out, so they could catch a glimpse or maybe talk to them.

Now *that* was strange, and it was a side effect of fame that they hadn't expected, and one they weren't comfortable with at all. It left no privacy. By then the cameras were long gone from the house, but there was no escaping the new celebrity. It was enough to make Sharon, at least, think that if they did another series, it would be filmed at their more isolated farm in England. The English, after all, were more reserved and wouldn't spend days waiting for them to emerge. Neither would they drive halfway across the country for a glimpse of the stars, as two girls from Colorado had done. When people in clubs went out of their way to tell Sharon how much they loved the show, or simply to brush against her so they could brag about it, things were getting decidedly weird and creepy.

But they'd chosen the territory, and now they had to live with it, as Ozzy had pointed out. Part of that was criticism. Some might be justified, a lot wouldn't be. Ozzy could ignore it—after all, he'd been called pretty much everything under the sun in his life—but Sharon couldn't. This was her brood, the people she loved with all her heart, and an attack on them wounded her deeply. She could even bite the hand that was feeding her: When mtv.com, the online arm of MTV, published something bad about Kelly's looks, Sharon was quick to go online and let loose with a broadside defense of her daughter. She could talk about her family, but no one else could. When she did it, it was with love.

HOW TO BE AN OZZY PARENT:

Defend your kids.

Perhaps Ozzy had the best idea, just lying back and letting things happen around him. Sharon and Kelly could go off on a spending spree with the gold card, and he could be horrified by how much they'd spent—but he was old enough and wise enough to realize that for a husband, discretion could be the better part of valor. Or when Sharon announced he'd just bought her a new car, accepting it was the easy way. Sometimes it was simply better and smarter for a husband to know when he was beaten.

HOW TO BE AN OZZY HUSBAND:

Know when to spend money on your wife.

But that didn't mean he was a pushover. He simply knew when to fight his battles and when to let things go. Also, he was happy to let Sharon be in control most of the time, to let her wear the pants in the house and lay down the law to the kids. It kept his life uncomplicated—and left more time to watch the History Channel. Still, he was already ready to offer his support and encouragement to all of them, and give his unconditional devotion. His home was his castle, and that was fine with him. He had his family and his things around him.

Life with the Osbournes

Sharon was always on top of things, to make sure things never veered too far out of hand.

"We definitely consulted with her on each episode," said MTV's Rod Aissa. "She's absolutely amazing in regard to handling business affairs, but also in capturing the trueness of who her husband is."

So there may be stuff that was never aired (*The Osbournes'* outtakes coming sometime, perhaps?); it seemed as if Sharon might have held a veto over material. If so, there was probably little she said no about. Viewers saw Ozzy deal with Jack over the issue of a knife that he wanted to carry with him one night. It had been a gift, and it was small, but Ozzy, for once, was completely adamant. He knew that if Jack was arrested, the whole family could end up deported—something he definitely didn't want to happen. And once he'd gotten the knife from his son, where was the best place to put it where a teenager wouldn't look for it? In the fruit bowl, of course.

So while some thought Ozzy simply bumbled around the house—his odd walk was just an effect of his medication—he could be as protective of his family as Sharon, wanting only the best for them. Like every parent, he'd lived more than his children, and did actually know a little bit more—like when it was time to get rid of Lola the bulldog, whose pet therapist visits he'd thought ridiculous, and who'd yet to be housebroken. It upset Jack, who owned Lola, but that was part of learning responsibility.

And both Kelly and Jack were much luckier than Ozzy himself. They didn't have to leave school at fifteen and begin work at menial jobs. They had the security of money behind them.

HOW TO BE AN OZZY PARENT:

Make a better life for your kids.

Money brought luxury. Like four stoves in the kitchen, although only one of them was ever used—and even then, not too often, it seemed. Once (as anyone who's seen *The Decline of Western Civilization Part Two: The Metal Years* knows) Ozzy liked the kitchen, especially making breakfast, but more recently he'd steered clear of cooking, claiming he'd "forgotten how." And in the kitchen, Sharon, he said, was "two-dimensional. It's either fantastic or a terrible f***ing disaster. She makes a great roast, though." But then again, Ozzy rarely ate red meat anymore, as part of his more-or-less vegetarian scheme. However, on the rare occasions he did cook, like his gravy at holiday dinner, he was over the moon that it had turned out well.

As Robert Thompson, director of the Center for the Study of Popular Television at Syracuse University in New York, pointed out, *The Osbournes* was "the first post-post-modern or post-post-ironic TV program." And what exactly did that mean? First of all, shows like *The Cosby Show, Leave It to Beaver,* or even *The Wonder Years* idealized the American nuclear family, seeing them through a rosy glow that had never been there in reality. In the nineties came a response, the dysfunctional families of *The Simpsons* and *Married with Children,* for example. And now, in the new millennium, there's Ozzy, a rock star who's completely himself, a total family man, and sometimes at the mercy of family forces around him.

All of which was fine for anyone who wanted to analyze, but the bottom line was that *The Osbournes* was incredibly entertaining, and hilarious television. It outdid even *The Real World* and *Beavis & Butthead* in terms of popularity for MTV, climbing to 6.3 million viewers, a record for the channel. They were American icons, which was an irony in itself, given that they were all English (although both Kelly and Jack sound completely American).

"I think that's kind of funny, when it's like 'America's family!' and meanwhile we have kind of a hard time getting to stay in the country!" said Jack. "So they love us so much—sling us a green card, if you will!"

That meant the Osbournes actually had no permanent resident status—they could be kicked out at any time—no wonder Ozzy was so paranoid about Jack carrying a knife!

And with the success of *The Osbournes,* the copycat ideas came springing out of the closet. There was talk about a similar reality show on rapper/label head Sean "P. Diddy" Combs, another on singer Brandy's pregnancy. Veteran rocker Alice Cooper offered himself. Dee Snider, who fronted the eighties metal band Twisted Sister, said he'd had a deal several years before for a rocker-at-home sitcom. *Extra,* the syndicated show, began doing at-home segments on Kiss tongue-man Gene Simmons and his nude-model wife, Shannon Tweed. You get something good, and everyone wants a piece of it.

But Ozzy was the original, and still the best. He had the name and the longevity—and the background of completely outrageous behavior to make the contrast. Plus he was Ozzy, lovable and witty in the natural way that couldn't be done otherwise without a good script.

"I think that a lot of people in this industry live a cliché rock-and-roll lifestyle," Sharon said on Fox News, "where they have—you know, I call them Versace rockers, you know, and you've got the perfect kids that become models or famous actresses, and you've got the perfect wife and the perfect husband that would never admit that they're addicted to anything, that would never admit that any of them are oversexed or whatever. They live a professional life, and then they have their private life. And we just are what we are."

They didn't talk down to their kids; they never had. They accepted that their kids would try things like alcohol, drugs, and sex, the way most kids do. And it would only be in extremes, where Ozzy and Sharon felt very strongly about something, that they'd finally say no.

HOW TO BE AN OZZY PARENT:

Always be truthful with your kids.

And what about Aimee, the daughter who'd opted out of the show to have her own life? At eighteen, she was older than her siblings, and didn't want her personal life invaded. Added to that, she was trying to get her own singing career off the ground. If she'd been part of the show, and had then been given a record deal, she'd never be sure if it was because of the show's success or her own talent. At least this way, she had her freedom and independence. And, as Sharon said, "she's the smart one out of the lot of us because she—she—she can walk down the street without anybody jumping on her, you know."

Aimee knew she didn't want her every move and word chronicled by cameras. But how was it for the others? How self-conscious were they about being filmed? For Ozzy, not at all. While the bedroom was understandably off limits, "sometimes I forget as soon as I open those doors that I'd be on. I would get kind of quick-tempered, you know, or surprised, forgetting they were there. And I would go, 'Not now, guys,' you know, and . . ."

But everything *was* on the record. Everything. The good times and the bad, although there were, in fact, very few bad times for the family. Jack and Kelly would argue, the way every brother and sister in the world does. But they'd also make up. And, perhaps most surprisingly, they'd often socialize together. In a way that almost mirrored their parents' relationship, Kelly was often the strong, together one, while Jack just tended to go with the flow.

The fact that they'd grown up in a wealthy family, with a privileged lifestyle, and a family name that everyone in music (and fandom) recognized, actually stood them in much better stead for the fame that came with the show. While they'd had a fair amount of anonymity before, and now it was gone, at least they'd had to deal before with people wanting to know them simply for who they were, related to not themselves. There might not have been the adulation, but at least they were prepared, and not about to naively accept just anybody. Jack had his small circle of close friends, and Kelly had her own friends, including singer and movie star Mandy Moore (whose mainstream cuteness might have seemed the opposite of Kelly, but they clicked on a girl level).

It was luck, and good judgment, that had brought MTV and one of the coolest families in America together. Really, the fact that they were English had little to do with anything, although the accent probably raised the cuteness factor for a lot of the audience (at least for those who could understand what Ozzy was saying).

"Family values" was an issue that had been in the forefront of American politics for a long time, and had been claimed by many different sides. To some it represented the traditional American values, the small-town, heartland America of the 1940s and 1950s, when everything was safe, and father, mother, and two children (or more) lived in a house with a white picket fence, and dinner was on the table when the father got home from work at six. The children could play safely outside, without any worries. To others, the family could be almost anything, a reflection of the high divorce rates and the number of single parents in the country.

It all depended on where you stood politically.

The beauty of the Osbournes was that they represented all sides of the family values issue. They could be incredibly liberal, with no real curfew set for their kids, and few limits on their behavior. At the same time, they were a very tight, loving unit, who spent a lot of time together. They could talk about things, and listen to each other. They fought, but they made up later. The father's job might not have been traditional, by any means, but the makeup of the family certainly was.

They crossed all the boundaries in a way no family on television had ever done before. They were hip, but the fact that Ozzy and Sharon had to be parents, deal with things, and set limits, also made them the more traditional kind of parent. They could be serious, but the sheer facts of their lives often took on ridiculous qualities. Used to dealing with contracts and concerts, Ozzy and Sharon could be confounded by the most basic things everyone took for granted, like the vacuum cleaner or getting the shrink wrap off a DVD.

When America watched *The Osbournes,* it was watching itself. That was one of the great factors in the show's popularity. Most might not have even realized it, let alone admitted it, but there's plenty of Ozzy in all of us. Maybe we don't walk like him, and most of us don't talk like him. We don't have his money, but we empathize with him, as life goes on around him, and sometimes the simple things become complicated. At home he's not Ozzy Osbourne the star, he's Ozzy the dad. He's taken off his rock'n'roll hat, the way most fathers take off their work clothes when they get home.

He's a man, not an icon. Most of us show one face to our colleagues at work, another to our friends, and when we're home, we're simply ourselves. That's what Ozzy shows on television. The manic stage personality vanishes, the Prince of Darkness turns on the lights and reveals his true self. And he's a cuddly Teddy bear of a man who wouldn't scare anyone. Especially his own children. For all the accoutrements around—like the Sodom and Gomorrah painting, the devil heads, and other assorted items associated with evil—he's actually a very meek man. And very moral, really—something most people would have refused to believe, if they hadn't seen it with their own eyes. But having gone through the immoral side, he's capable of speaking with authority—although he's not one to lecture at all.

But he doesn't need to. His kids have seen his life. They remember when he was an alcoholic, and running out of control. They've waved him off to rehab more than once. And now they have him back, whole—at least, when he's not on tour, which isn't as often as it used to be; age has slowed him down a little.

He and Sharon have allowed their children to grow up as individuals. Yes, they're perfectly normal teenagers in many ways, but there's also a maturity about them that's developed because they've become themselves. They haven't felt the need to conform to any clique, or be a part of any social group. That's something that will stand them in good stead for the future, whatever they decide to do (and it's unlikely that Kelly will try and follow her sister into a singing career).

Really, though, neither Sharon nor Ozzy is likely to push the kids in any direction. They respect their children too much for that. Above all they want to see them happy in their lives, no matter what they do. A lot of parents give lip service to that idea, but never apply it in their own families. But having lived an unconventional life, they don't need to impose anything on their children—and the kids themselves haven't reacted by turning conventional (as in the sitcom *Family Ties,* where Michael J. Fox, as the son, reacted to his liberal parents by becoming ultraconservative).

Something they know, that all parents come to learn sooner or later, is that there are no hard and fast rules about being a parent. There can't be; situations change so quickly, and you have to adapt. So many have learned the hard way about that. But most parents are making it all up as they go along (they simply don't tell that to their kids). Of course, there have to be limits; that's a given for any part of life. Ozzy and Sharon have established those boundaries, and though Jack and Kelly will butt heads against them, and they can tell their parents to f*** off, they stay within them. They're good kids who've been raised well. They're well-adjusted, able to deal with anything that happens. Maybe they're a bit spoiled materially, but no more so than anyone else from a wealthy family. And they're remarkably supportive of each other. To attack one is to have the other instantly leap to the defense, far more than in most families.

THE OSBOURNES QUIZ, PART TWO

1. Who, according to Sharon, runs the house?

2. What kind of gravy did Ozzy make?

3. Where did he hide Jack's knife?

4. What T-shirt was Jack wearing that Ozzy objected to?

5. Ozzy rescued one of the family cats on the final episode—where was it trapped?

6. What did Ozzy use to demonstrate to the family the stress fracture in his leg?

7. What other family member had to wear a cast?

8. Which of the kids has a fake I.D.?

9. Who made Kelly's appointment with the "vagina doctor"?

10. What infection has Kelly never had?

OZZY QUIZ: ANSWERS

1. Minnie the dog, also known as the queen of metal

2. Turkey gravy

3. In the fruit bowl

4. A picture of the late John Belushi, with the word cocaine

5. Behind a desk mirror

6. A loaf of bread

7. Kelly

8. Kelly

9. Her older sister Aimee

10. A yeast infection

HOW TO BE AN OZZY PARENT:

Be prepared to improvise.

So while the love might not be immediately apparent, it's the bedrock of everything they do. It's the glue that keeps them together through the bad times and the good, and it's the reason Ozzy says he couldn't live without Sharon, and why the family is his entire life. Many men might think it, but few would be open enough to come out and say that to the faces of those around them, and allow themselves to be that vulnerable.

To think of Ozzy, the metal god, as a "new man" might seem absurd, but he is, really. He's sensitive and caring, even though he can zone out from the family arguments, as he's been known to do. To be fair, Ozzy can sometimes seem like he's zoned out from the world, and occasionally has a kind of cocoon around him. That's simply the manner he's developed over the years. And he's no different from many other middle-aged males, confused by new technology that seems like second nature to the kids. He's just a man.

"I've had kids come up to me at Ozzfest, saying 'Ozzy's bigger than God.' I'm not bigger than God. I'm just a guy who's had a great gift of entertainment bestowed upon him. And I'm just trying to let them know that I bleed, too. I worry, too. I have my issues, therapy, sleepless nights. I worry about my children's futures."

He's proud of his house, that he and Sharon have been able to buy something like a mansion in Beverly Hills. For all the pop star dreams he had when he was young, he never expected anything like this, or to still be in the music business after thirty-four years, a man with the Midas touch, bigger than ever.

Ultimately, it was the classic story of a family moving in and adjusting to life in a new neighborhood, and coping with the little everyday problems and the kids. Were the Osbournes just the Simpsons in 3-D form, as some have suggested? There could be a cartoon element to it, and a sitcom element, too (part *Leave It to Beaver,* part *The Honeymooners,* perhaps?). But it was real life. And although reality television wasn't as popular as it had been a couple of years earlier, when *Survivor* and the like took all the ratings, a new twist—especially one which offered both humor and a peek into the lives of celebrities—was bound to be popular.

We all want to see how the other half lives, and to be able to laugh at their failings and foibles. The nature of fame is to put people on pedestals, and make them larger than life. But we also want to see the pedestals crumble, to remember that they're flesh and blood, and put their pants on one leg at a time, the same as the rest of us.

But while you could laugh at Ozzy trying to convince Kelly to go to the gynecologist, you could also laugh *with* him. The situations that came up were everyday and mundane. Yes, it was almost surreal to find a rock star whose reputation rests on loud riffs and metal madness trying to figure out how to work the remote or the vacuum cleaner—but how many men hadn't been in the same situation at one time or another? We could relate, and laugh at ourselves, too. How many of us hadn't wanted to curse in those situations? Most of us restrained ourselves, usually because the kids were around. For Ozzy, swearing was such a part of his vocabulary that it was simply there, it had lost its power. It didn't shock, it was simply a part of him.

That was true of the whole family, of course. Sharon and the kids didn't exactly censor themselves, either. But it was one of the charming little quirks that made the Osbournes into the Osbournes, and they wouldn't have been the same without it.

He's fifty-three, but young enough inside to remember what it's like to be a teenager—you could say he's made his living from being a perpetual teenager (and given that Ozzfest took in the best part of $40 million in the last two years alone, he's done it very, very well). He's pushed down more boundaries with outrage in his time than most people could imagine, which makes him generally well qualified to deal with a pair of teenagers, especially his son, when Jack gets it into his head that he doesn't have to obey anyone and go to school. It's like rock'n'roll.

"Someone says you can't listen to that, listen to this, and you can bet your a** the first chance a kid gets, he's going to listen to the stuff he's told not to listen to."

Even if it's not thought out, all child rearing is psychology. Ozzy just happens to be a natural at it. He makes mistakes, but every parent in the world has—many times over. But whether they rebel or not, Jack and Kelly know he loves them in an unconditional way—and they love him back.

He's stuck in the past, to an extent (he'll listen to Creed, for example, but most of the music on MTV does nothing for him; he's first and foremost a Beatles fan, and will always be so). But at fifty-three, that's only to be expected. And let's face it, his job and stature make him hipper than most parents on the planet, even if it's largely killed his hearing—but every job has its drawbacks.

There *should* be a generation gap between parents and children. Each generation needs to think it's inventing sin, and pushing further. But when you've got a father who's already done it all, how can that happen?

Perhaps because he *has* done it all, and he knows the dangers of excess, having lived them. So when he says no, he means it, and he says it for a reason. Not because it's "bad," as many people might say it, but because it can be dangerous—the tattoos and knives, for example.

And he was brought up to be polite, to respect his elders. It was the way of life in the Britain of his childhood. And while neither Jack nor Kelly might show obvious respect (certainly, telling your father to f*** off isn't obvious respect), they do listen when he lays down the law, because they know he means it. Usually it's Sharon setting the rules, and while she can be playful, they also understand she takes no nonsense—if she says something, she wants it done. She's businesslike, and brooks no refusal. And they've learned that over the years.

So when Sharon said Jack's houseguest had to go, he knew the time was up. She'd put her foot down, and that was it.

And, like all parents, they didn't want too much noise in the house. The kids played their music too loud. They left messes. These were universal complaints. They just happened to be heard in a $4.5 million mansion in Beverly Hills instead of an apartment or a subdivision in the suburbs. The words echoed, not just through America, but around the world.

Which is why *The Osbournes* has global appeal. It's been shown in the U.S. and Canada, and has begun airing in Britain. For every English-speaking country (perhaps especially Britain, where they

THE OZZY FACT FILE

1. *Born John Michael Osbourne in Aston, Birmingham, England, on December 3, 1948.*

2. *Has sung with Black Sabbath and led his own band.*

3. *Has released fifteen solo albums (including greatest hits packages), and seven with Sabbath.*

4. *Managed by Sharon Osbourne.*

5. *Famous for biting the head off a dove in his record company office, and the head off a bat onstage.*

6. *Arrested for urinating on the Alamo while wearing his wife's dress.*

7. *Now completely clean and sober, works out every day, and no longer smokes.*

8. *Every one of his solo albums has sold at least a million copies.*

9. *Acknowledged as the godfather of heavy metal.*

10. *Always the star of Ozzfest, the touring festival which is now in its seventh year, and remains one of the highest-grossing musical events in the U.S.*

11. Has six children—two from his first marriage (plus one adopted), and three from his second marriage. Estranged from Jessica, the daughter of his first marriage.

12. Married twice. Currently to Sharon, for twenty years.

13. Musical heroes: The Beatles.

14. Apart from being a singer, he's worked in a slaughter-house, as a car horn tester, and as a plumber's apprentice.

15. Has been in jail several times, the first occasion being for burglary, when he was seventeen.

could understand Ozzy's accent more easily than some Americans) it was a natural, a reflection of life. Prior to the show being seen in the U.K., Ozzy was all over the papers and television.

The show made the entire family into celebrities. They were on the cover of *Rolling Stone, Entertainment Weekly,* and more than a handful of other magazines. Rosie O'Donnell was a huge fan, as she frequently announced on her show. Jay Leno loved having Ozzy and Sharon on his talk show.

Ozzy had been in the limelight for three decades, but this was different. For most of that time his fame had been limited to music circles, except for his more outrageous exploits. Now he was part of the establishment, the mainstream media. They loved the family. But why? In part, because the show was so successful. But also because they were something fresh, not manufactured. In a world where Britney, 'NSync, and movie stars were the main currency of celebrity, the Osbournes were a breath of really fresh air. And it was a great story, too—which never hurt. Ozzy's colorful past, and its relative contrast with the present, offered plenty of scope for journalists. And Ozzy's openness in interviews—possibly the result of many visits to his therapist—provided great copy.

Ozzy as father of the year might have seemed strange. But it wasn't, really. He made time for his children, in a way many fathers couldn't or didn't. He wasn't afraid of being physical with his affection, of hugging Kelly to reassure her, or snogging with his wife backstage at *The Tonight Show*. He was tolerant and happy, rarely in a bad mood, and very even-tempered—when he was angry, it was obvious, and a warning sign. He indulged his kids (he didn't need to indulge Sharon, she could manage that by herself), but also knew where to draw the line.

If his professional life is a fantasy come true—and let's face it, most people have had the fantasy of being rock stars, with all the privileges, at one time or another—then his home life is reality, and a place where he's completely comfortable. His every wish isn't granted by someone else there, he takes on a lot of the responsibility, even if trash bags can be a problem sometimes. But he's lucky; his children understand both sides of his life. They've gone on tour with him often enough, and seen what that side of his life is like (how many fathers really take their kids to work with them?), and they've experienced it properly—Jack even had a drill put up his nose in the Ozzfest sideshow a couple of years ago.

And that's fine. They need to experiment, to keep redefining their limits, and on tour is a surprisingly safe atmosphere, like a cocoon. And at Ozzfest, all the other bands look after the kids—it's like an extended family on the road, with Ozzy as the father figure and Sharon as everyone's den mother.

At home, too, Sharon had the den mother's role, but with assistance from Melinda, who, while she didn't have much authority with Jack at times, had backup from both Ozzy and Sharon. To sass Melinda was to incur Ozzy's wrath.

But there was plenty to share, too. Jack, a huge fan of Tool, saw them play with King Crimson, a band that had begun around the same time as Black Sabbath. Jack liked King Crimson, and told Ozzy, who then suggested he listen to a couple of other prog bands from that era—Yes and Gentle Giant—which Jack enjoyed, to his surprise. So there were still little bonding rituals to be undergone, and things Ozzy could teach his son.

The one rule that no one was allowed to break was no smoking in the house. Outside was fine, but not inside. Sharon was quite content to let the kids have parties at the house, though—after all, that way she could monitor what was going on, and there was no drinking and driving risk for the kids.

They were kids, and they'd make mistakes. Sharon and Ozzy both knew that, and accepted it. As long as they weren't busted for something (Ozzy's great fear seemed to be getting deported from the U.S.), it was fine, mistakes were normal. Both the parents, especially Ozzy, had made plenty in their own time.

"I think a big part of being a parent is to be there when your kids f*** up. You pick them up, dust them off, and try to put them back on the right road. But all kids want to experiment, all kids are gonna break their curfews, that's part of being a kid."

To be fair, Sharon didn't mind too much if they broke curfews, as long as they called and let her know what was happening. That didn't mean she'd sleep—she couldn't, until they were both home and in bed (whatever their ages, they were still her babies).

They wanted their kids to try hard at school, but they had no expectations of them being top students; not everyone can be. As long as they did their best, and made the effort, that was all they could ask. And they could tell when the kids were holding back on the truth, or lying; that was simply being a parent. They did a lot of things, and spent a lot of time, together. That helped Ozzy and Sharon see right through anything their kids might tell them.

HOW TO BE AN OZZY PARENT:

Never expect your kids to be perfect students.
Simply ask that they do their best.

One thing Sharon did insist on was that Jack have respect for women. That was vitally important. In the rock world, women, especially the groupies, were often simply seen as commodities. And his name (and since the show, his status) meant there would always be girls willing to have sex with him, just for who he was. She wanted him to think, and not just take the easy option and use available girls. There was more to sex than that, and it was something vital to remember.

Of course, Jack could find talking about sex with his mother to be "awkward," but what teenage boy wouldn't be embarrassed by that? Still, it wasn't as bad as her flashing her boobs in front of one of his friends, as she did once, or Ozzy walking around in his underwear.

But one thing the kids could always agree on was the fact that their parents were cool. That was because they were willing to take the time to talk and to listen.

"Whether they do anything about it is another thing, but they still take the time to talk to me," Kelly said. "There are too many parents that don't talk to their kids. And if they do, it's like telling them something instead of reasoning with them."

They've acquired a balance that eludes most families. They don't sweat the small stuff, and they've learned that most things are quite small—even the major things, most of the time.

That's what comes across. They don't need to try hard to be good parents, to put on a show for the cameras. It's the way they've always been, natural and easy. There's a warmth and camaraderie in their house; all of them are at ease with themselves and each other. Even when there's tension, it soon passes, and the normal rhythm of life resumes.

Sharon

Many people think of Sharon Osbourne as the brains of the family. She's certainly the organized one, and she largely runs the household, making sure it ticks along as smoothly as an Osbourne household can—which isn't always that smoothly. As Ozzy's wife of twenty years, she probably knows him better than anyone, and loves him with a complete devotion.

She's experienced a lot, both as his wife and his manager, in the time they've been together, which began in the late seventies. She's nurtured his career, guided it, while letting him run free and wild, and he's always come back to her. She's tolerated his excesses, and seen him give them all up.

She's also one of the few powerful women in the music business, the manager of someone who's remained one of the top concert draws for many, many years. Along with Ozzy, she runs her own label, Divine, and has signed several bands. She's managed a number of artists, and in the rough and tumble world of the music business has earned respect. Possibly only Susan Silver, who looked after the careers of Alice in Chains and Soundgarden, approached a similar stature, but even she didn't come close.

But Sharon cut her teeth in the music business. Her father, Don Arden, had been one of the first powerful managers in Britain, beginning in the 1950s and the dawn of rock'n'roll. Born in 1956, it surrounded her from the time she was born. He looked after rocker Gene Vincent in Europe, as well as others, such as Chuck Berry.

Rock'n'roll died after British bands like the Beatles took off, and Arden was quick to keep pace. In 1965 he began working with the Small Faces, helping them become one of the top pop acts in the U.K., although, in retrospect, they felt as if he'd underpaid them for their work.

Arden's hard image increased when, in 1966, he allegedly threatened another up-and-coming manager, Robert Stigwood, with being thrown out of a window for trying to steal away the Small Faces.

From there, he moved up, managing the Move from 1968, then taking on their offshoot band, the Electric Light Orchestra, who'd become massive during the seventies. He started his own successful label, Jet, and managed Black Sabbath (who, like the Move and ELO, came from Birmingham), bringing Sharon and her brother, David, into his company.

While Sharon split from her father under very bad terms, David continued to work for him—at least until 1986, when he ended up in prison. Don, though acquitted on other charges, had been ground down by legal fees and largely retired, shuttling between his homes in Beverly Hills and Surrey.

Sharon began her working life as a receptionist at her father's company, which was how she met Ozzy. But their relationship became much closer after he was fired from Sabbath in 1979, and she helped him find his feet as a solo act, introducing him to guitarist Randy Rhoads.

She's never been reserved, and always outspoken for (and about) the artists she's managed. While Ozzy's been her prime focus, and these days her only one, over the course of her career she's also managed guitarist Gary Moore (who's been successful in Europe), former Runaway turned metal guitarist/singer Lita Ford (with whom Ozzy enjoyed a top ten single), the Quireboys (an English act who appeared on the brink of success, then disappeared, and dark metallers Coal Chamber. There was also a celebrated stint managing Smashing Pumpkins. That lasted all of three months, before Sharon famously handed in her resignation, for "medical reasons—Billy Corgan is making me sick!"

She reportedly kneed a promoter in the groin when he was slow to pay what he owed, and on another occasion walked into the office of a company selling illegal merchandise and trashed their computer system before walking out—only to return because she'd left her car keys.

Sharon had Ozzy arrested in 1989 when, in an alcoholic daze, he tried to strangle her. But what could have been the end brought a reconciliation, because, she said "I admire him and I love him."

Sharon's reputation for toughness, however, has always been different from her father's. Quite definitely, she's never been someone to mess with or take lightly because she's a woman (a mistake several have made over the years), but she can be aggressive simply because she defends her clients—and most especially Ozzy—as if she were a lioness looking after her young. Artists still come to her for advice, and asking her to manage them. In recent years she's turned down Fred Durst of Limp Bizkit, Guns N'Roses, and Courtney Love to be able to focus on Ozzy and Ozzfest.

She's driven to succeed, a workaholic who can easily survive on four or five hours a night (probably just as well, because that's all she usually manages to get). From being derided, she's won respect, most particularly for Ozzfest, which took in almost $40 million in the last two years alone, and has proved to be by far the most successful and enduring of the traveling festivals.

But between Ozzy and the festival, there's plenty to keep her busy. She made a deliberate choice not to manage any other artists after run-ins with them—they simply didn't want to hear the truths she had to tell them, and she's never been one to wrap them in cotton wool. If they couldn't take what she had to tell them, they had no business being her clients.

And yes, she can anger easily at times, and go over the top (witness the ham incident, for example). But her own times of excess, when she and Ozzy used to go over the top together, are long in the past. While she could say "Our fights were legendary"—he'd rush offstage during guitar solos to fight with her, then back on to finish his vocal—she knew that things couldn't last that way, and motherhood as well as business provided the catalyst for her to tone down.

She's a person who quite naturally takes charge of things, an organizer, so it's no surprise she runs the house and the family. She can multitask quite easily, keeping her fingers in several projects at once—and still finding time to read her pile of magazines (Sharon loves magazines). She's the real disciplinarian, the one who keeps everything in hand. And she's never been afraid to admonish her kids. There was an incident, several years ago, when she discovered her children sniggering at a group of Ozzy fans. She took them to task right then and there, pointing out that those were the people who allowed them to enjoy their lifestyle, and they needed to respect them.

Respect is an important word to her. She wants Jack to respect women, for example, and for herself, she's earned respect in the music business. She knows she's had to work extra hard for that respect, simply because she's a woman, and in music, even more than other areas of business, women are looked on as second-class citizens. As she pointed out, "If you're a woman and you say no in business, they call you a b****. If you say yes, you get s*** on."

She looks at life with her eyes wide open, there's no doubt about that. She's had to work and fight hard for her stature. If she and Ozzy had received the respect she thought due, there might never have been an Ozzfest; she only started it because the Lollapalooza organizers turned Ozzy down for not being cool enough. The new festival was her revenge on them. It simply turned into something much bigger than she could have anticipated.

Sharon's a very smart woman. She likes her luxuries—the good house, the nice car, fancy clothes, and regular hair appointments. But she's earned them all, and she's dedicated her life to her husband, and made quite sure the kids were included every step of the way. They've gone on tour with their parents, been a part of Ozzfest—almost the mascots at times, or so it's seemed—

SHARON OSBOURNE
FACT FILE

1. *Born 1956, London, England*

2. *Daughter of manager Don Arden*

3. *First met Ozzy in 1974, when she was eighteen*

4. *Began managing Ozzy in the late seventies, became his full manager in the early eighties after buying his contract from her dad for $1.5 million*

5. *Responsible for the start of Ozzfest in 1996*

6. *Mother of three children—Aimee, 18, Kelly, 17, Jack, 16.*

7. *Married Ozzy July 4, 1982 in Hawaii*

8. *Also managed Lita Ford, Coal Chamber, Quireboys, Gary Moore, and Smashing Pumpkins*

9. *Now living in the twenty-fourth house she and Ozzy have owned*

10. *Lost ninety-five pounds by having a band inserted around her stomach to make it smaller*

11. *Allegedly kneed a promoter in the groin to get payment of money due*

12. *Has never let her father see his grandchildren*

13. *Co-owns the Divine record label with Ozzy*

14. *Loves to shop*

15. *Not addicted to designer labels*

and seen what happens in their lives almost from the time they were born.

Sharon also used to be a great deal larger than she is today. The svelte woman of *The Osbournes* is relatively recent. In 1999 she underwent an operation intended to shrink her stomach by inserting a band around it. It worked; she went from 224 pounds down to 129 pounds—a remarkable 95-pound weight loss. But at five feet two, it probably made her healthier. Still, she's rarely been self-conscious. She did admit that when the cameras were first rolling at home, she primped a little. But after a while, when they became an accepted part of daily life, she stopped thinking about it and reverted to her normal self, not caring about makeup or hair. But she didn't need to. The dynamo with plenty of warmth came through however she looked.

She was always protective of her clients (especially Ozzy, quite naturally), but with her family she's positively fierce. To criticize them in any way is to incur her wrath. And while she might be a kinder, gentler Sharon these days, once her temper flares, it's better to watch out, as a reporter discovered when asking if the series would be close-captioned for those who couldn't understand Ozzy's thick Birmingham accent. Or just ask the neighbors who played music too loud. Messing with Sharon is a way to bite off more than you can chew.

And she can be incredibly playful, too. She's not averse to gleefully flashing her boobs at her son's friends and asking if they think she's sexy (not exactly the action of an introvert), or having a laugh of any kind. Unlike her husband, she's out a lot, usually in clubs, listening to bands and doing business.

But before *The Osbournes* she enjoyed relative anonymity. People in the business knew her, and bands knew. Now she's a national figure, and that doesn't always sit well with her.

"People started stopping us in the street after the first week," she recalled, "asking about the house and the animals. Yesterday people were screaming at us on the street, and I was only out to buy a pair of tights."

So fame does have its drawbacks, but it's also made Sharon into a full-fledged celebrity, almost as famous as her husband, appearing with Rosie O'Donnell, on CNBS's *Business Center,* and the *Today Show,* as well as being featured in network television specials revolving around Mother's Day.

From June Cleaver to Sharon Osbourne might seem almost as big a leap as from Ward to Ozzy, but it all makes sense. She's a woman who can call her daughter Topsy and poppet, but she can also be merciless with them goading and teasing before relenting and being a loving mom.

And a devoted pet owner, too. Sharon loves having her dogs around, even when they don't behave as well as they should. Ozzy, it seems, tolerates them; Sharon's the one who has the true affection for them.

Maybe she's not as crazy as her husband, but she can be as wicked, and as foul-mouthed. While her language is second nature to her now, she can moderate it socially—if she has to. And it does give her the appearance of toughness, although she can be a soft sweetie when she lets her guard down. The tough image is a shell she's had to develop professionally.

Of course, that doesn't stop her from trading quips with Ozzy, and speaking to him on his own level, even when he can get base. She knows that he's just using words, and they don't mean anything. He loves her, he's utterly devoted and dependent on her, and she understands him on every level—which is why she enjoys seeing him on the show, noting that "What's so funny is that people in America don't understand a single word he's saying. They don't even understand his body language."

America—and now plenty of other parts of the world—might have peeked inside the lives and the rooms of the Osbournes, but they could never understand them the way Sharon did. She lived with them in a way the viewers couldn't, even when the crew tried to sneak a little extra.

". . . they put a camera in our bedroom," she said, "and I made them take it out. Then they put it back in again."

Needless to say, Sharon won that battle. She won all the battles—but she was used to fighting and negotiation, and very little fazed her (and a woman who could go off on-camera was something to be feared).

She's an original, and they broke the mold after they made her. She keeps all the sides of her life in balance, and manages to look elegant even when she's being bleeped—and between them, the family managed to be bleeped every nineteen seconds (on average) during the show. She's mentioned before that everyone used to expect Ozzy to wheel out the standard centerfold trophy wife—which she knows she's not. But there's a resilience to her that goes far below the skin, and a beauty, too.

Her word is law in the house. That applies to everyone, even Ozzy. She'll let him go so far, but then she'll yank on his leash, just as she will with the kids. But, like Ozzy, she's willing to trust the kids a lot, and let them learn from their mistakes, the way she and her husband did.

Still, when she says no, and raises her voice, they know she means business. About the only ones who can ignore her then are the dogs (and sometimes at their own peril).

HOW TO BE AN OZZY PARENT:

Your wife is always right. Even when she's not.

She loves to spend money, but she and Ozzy make enough, so it's no problem—they're not likely to go broke in this life. And she likes working on the interior decoration of the houses. As Kelly put it, "She has an 'I need to decorate' thing, but it's Martha Stewart on crack." Which might be a little unfair—Sharon has wide taste, and good taste, and she's always been very hands-on. She might not make the draperies, but she chose them herself, and didn't rely on some interior designer. Of course, given the eclectic nature of their paintings and other things, it might have been impossible to find one who could accommodate them.

Just as her father brought her into the family business, she seems to be bringing Jack along. Although he works for Epic, he discusses the bill for Ozzfest with Sharon, and she listens to his suggestions—it was his idea to include Meshuggah, Soil, and Adema on this year's list. It's quite possible that soon it'll be Osbourne and Son, and the list of bands managed will expand from just Ozzy to include more of Jack's taste. Will Sharon be ready to hand off some of the responsibility, after working alone for so long? Well, technically not alone, since she does have an office and a staff—neither of which are at home—but she's never worked with any kind of business partner since striking out on her own.

It's beyond doubt that Sharon's happy with her life and, most especially, her family. They're her stability and her safe harbor, but in a different way to Ozzy. They give her energy, and center her. There's banter, words back and forth, small arguments and crises, but it's much better than business because, at the end of the day, there's plenty of love. And they need her just as much as she needs them around her to make everything sane again. None of the money or the fame can compare with that. She values what they've earned, but her family is priceless. It might not be quite the normal nuclear family of American tradition. Or then again, maybe the Osbournes are simply redefining what the nuclear family really is in the new millennium.

The Kids

Jack, Kelly, and Aimee are a handful. In other words, they're like most teenagers. While no one who watches *The Osbournes* has seen Aimee, completely by her own choice, they've seen plenty of Jack and Kelly.

KELLY

She's got a punk haircut of uncertain and often-changing color. She argues with her brother and gets embarrassed by her parents when they show each other affection. She's ready to be grown up and tough sometimes, but on other occasions she's like a little girl. It can only be one thing—a teenage girl.

At seventeen, Kelly Osbourne (born October 27, 1984) is on the cusp. A girl who's almost a woman, and trying to find her place in the world. She doesn't follow fashion, making up her own style as she goes along. Perhaps because of the life she's lived, moving so

THE KELLY FILE

1. *Born October 27, 1984*

2. *Close friend: Mandy Moore*

3. *Wants to live in New York someday*

4. *Spent part of* The Osbournes *in a cast after hurting her leg*

5. *Most famous show incidents: the tattoo, the faked ID, losing a credit card*

6. *Most traumatic experience? Watching the Twin Towers fall*

7. *Overall favorite band? Incubus*

8. *Favorite way of passing time? Hanging out in clubs with friends, making fun of celebrities*

9. *Embarrassed by? Her father in his underwear, her mother flashing, her parents showing affection to each other*

10. *Most frequently disobeyed house rule? Curfew*

often, and frequently on the road with her parents, she doesn't have many close friends.

No one ever said growing up was easy. But with a close family, and parents she can trust—when they don't make her blush—Kelly is lucky, and she realizes it.

Being a vital part of *The Osbournes* has been a learning experience for her, to see herself, every action, speech, and mistake preserved on screen for the world to know all about.

At first, the novelty of being on MTV, a channel she'd grown up watching, was appealing. But when she realized just how much of her life had become public property, she was far less comfortable with the whole idea.

"It feels like I've had my life signed away, and no one informed me about it," she said.

One item that's come up regularly in chatrooms and on notice boards about Kelly is her weight. Strangers have stopped her to discuss it, people have written about it in disparaging terms.

"I'm not fat and I'm not thin," she announced. "And I'm not trying to be a f***ing supermodel, so I wish people would just leave it alone."

Many teenage girls have image problems with their weight; that's just the way society makes them think. But she seems comfortable with herself, and the bottom line is that's what matters. Others will always say what they want, and some, like Sharon, will leap to their daughters' defense. But as long as the girl's comfortable, that's what counts.

HOW TO BE AN OZZY PARENT:

Always support your children, make them feel wanted and secure, and happy with themselves as they are.

For now she doesn't appear to have too many goals in life, but that's fine—she's only seventeen, and there's no need to make a decision about the future yet. The closest she's come to a plan is singing "Papa Don't Preach" on the soundtrack of *The Osbournes*, accompanied by two members of Incubus.

"I'm kind of crapping myself because I don't think I'm a very good singer," she admitted, but from all reports, the demo version she did sounded just fine. The only drawback, as far as she's concerned, is that the album will be produced by Jack. She has enough contact with her little brother as it is, without him being in charge of her in a recording studio.

Could it be a singing career's ahead of her? Probably not, especially when her older sister Aimee (who also takes charge of Kelly by making gynecologist appointments for her) is looking to break into that field.

Really, she's simply trying to find herself. That's one reason she got the tattoo on her hip that caused such a fuss, or why she's frequently embarrassed by the antics of her parents. Maybe she looks a little different at times, but she's a perfectly normal teenager. And that includes using her fake ID to get into clubs (which isn't as easy now that her face is nationally known).

Perhaps understandably, she has a very close relationship with her mother. The two of them can go shopping together (and they can also keep a secret about a lost credit card), and have fun in a way she never can with Ozzy, for example. But the mother-daughter conversations have always been open. As a family they listen to each other (well, when anyone can get a word in edgewise), and attempt to talk things out, which is healthy for the kids.

And she and Jack are close, too, in a way most brothers and sisters can't manage, perhaps because they've been thrown into each other's company so much when growing up. They often hang out together. They argue, quite naturally, but always make up; there's no ongoing feud between them, the way some families seem to manage. She feels responsible for him. She's the one who'll go and pick him up when he's in trouble, because he's her little brother.

Like Sharon, Kelly is very together. She's not afraid to confront the world head-on. And she's not afraid to swear at it, either. She's inherited her vocabulary from her parents, and while some of it might be deliberately designed to shock ("Can you be arrested for calling someone a c**t?" for example), most of it is without a second thought. It's just the way the Osbournes punctuate their speech and make their points, and she's very much an Osbourne.

For all the craziness of the house, she's very well-adjusted. She's tolerant, at least to a point, but push her a little too far, and she'll snap back at anyone, even her parents. It's not an act for the cameras or the press, this is the way she really is. But she has a tender side, and can open up a little when she's out with girlfriends like singer/actress Mandy Moore.

She's eager to please fans who want a picture taken with her, but

YOU DON'T KNOW JACK

1. *Born November 8, 1985*

2. *The only son in the family*

3. *Favorite band? Tool*

4. *Most famous series incident? The knife and Lola*

5. *Favorite thing to do? Hang out with friends*

6. *Biggest passion? Music*

7. *Is he really surly? No*

8. *Current part-time job? Scouting bands for Epic*

9. *Favorite pet? Lola the bulldog*

10. *Favorite word? You mean you can't guess it?*

easily annoyed by their intrusions into her privacy. She'd like to have it all, but she's realizing that she can't, and it's hard. Of course, she had no idea the show would become so big, and that there'd be fans crowding around the gates of the house. Sharon had guessed it would be a cult thing, like the outrageous British sit-com *Absolutely Fabulous* (although the Osbournes are actually decidedly more functional), and there was no reason for anyone in the family to think otherwise.

But like it or not, Kelly's a celebrity now. America knows her, or thinks it does. But underneath the language is a girl who can be quite prudish, who's not comfortable talking about sex with her parents, and who was brought up to be basically polite. (". . . if I say anything it's 'Mom, you're being a b****' and it doesn't go any farther than that. And it's only out of anger.")

HOW TO BE AN OZZY PARENT:

Let your kids vent their anger and frustration at you sometimes. It's healthy and it's safe. And it's only words; as soon as they're spoken, the feelings are gone.

But she's a cool girl, too, with her own sense of fashion that doesn't follow any kind of trend. She might shop at Fred Segal, the upscale L.A. department store, but she puts her outfits together in a very individual way, as she always has. Both Ozzy and

Sharon have encouraged her to be that way, and it shows in all sides of her life.

HOW TO BE AN OZZY PARENT:

Let your kids be themselves in fashion. In some ways it's a lot better if they don't follow the crowd.

She's as comfortable crying at *A Walk to Remember* (and not just because her friend Mandy Moore was in it), or listening loudly to the Strokes, a retro-style garage band. In time she'd love to live in New York, a place halfway between California and England (as she put it), and where the people are more real than L.A. Which is important, because Kelly is never anything less than real. She remains a huge Incubus fan (which is why cutting a track with two of them is so special), but can't name an all-time favorite CD.

Like all teenagers, she's going through a lot of changes and constantly growing. She's good at science and history, but hates math with a passion—she simply can't see the point of it.

Even if she can't see it yet, the future's wide open ahead of her. She's luckier than most. Not many girls her age get to travel around the world—this year she's already been to Japan and Korea, and she'll be in England in June—and see the things she's seen (there's also a family joke that Ozzy's bought her a house in

China; don't expect her to visit it anytime soon). Quite what she'll end up doing remains to be seen—she doesn't have Jack's passion for music, for example. And there's a fair chance she'll go on to college before making any decisions, although the show will make her an instant celebrity in the dorm room, too—at least until all the other girls become comfortable with her. She'll grow at her own pace, and neither Ozzy nor Sharon are likely to put any pressure on her to do anything else.

HOW TO BE AN OZZY PARENT:

Let your children grow at their own pace. They're individuals, and they have to develop as themselves. Square pegs won't go into round holes, no matter how much you force them.

JACK

At sixteen, Jack's the Osbourne baby. Of course, he doesn't see it like that, but to his parents, and even his older sisters, that's exactly what he is. Even if his hair is dyed blond, or shaved (as happened at Ozzfest a couple of years ago), or in a Mohawk, they can all see the little boy underneath.

Jack's growing up, however. He already has a job, working for

Epic Records as a scout, and helping his mother with Ozzfest. He's strongly focused on music, and while it's not his entire life, it's a great portion of it. With stickers for the band Tool all over his bedroom door, he's got it bad for that band. His favorite artist, his favorite all-time concert—you could call him a Toolhead. But, being so involved with music, he's taken the time to analyze why they put on such a great show, and what makes their albums so good.

The very nature of the job he has, scouting bands for the Epic record label (it's a part-time job, and a lot better and more glamorous than stacking carts in the supermarket), has him out in the clubs a lot, quite often with his mother—and how many teenagers would be seen dead in a club with their mom? But she knows the business and the people even better than he does, and he can learn a lot from her.

When he's not out and about, he's usually hanging out with friends, exactly the way all teenagers do. Often that's at his house, in part because he has the room, and parents who won't complain too much if the music's loud, as long as it doesn't go on too late. He's in no hurry to move out, in part because the house has everything he needs (without paying rent), but also because his friends live close by.

HOW TO BE AN OZZY PARENT:

Indulge your children a little. They grow up too quickly.

He doesn't have a big group of friends—being the son of a celebrity has made him a bit wary and cynical. But he's very close to the ones he does have.

Jack was the one who came up with the idea for the show, but he's become the one who dislikes it most. It's intruded on his life in ways he never imagined, not only through the fans who won't give the family any peace at home, but also in some of the things that have been shown. After all, most teenage boys don't have their family fights shown to the world, and when you're trying to establish yourself, it can be a bit humiliating. But he seems to have come through with his self-esteem intact, although his cynicism is a bit stronger that it was before (which is saying quite a bit). After all, he recalled, "There was a camera in my bedroom the whole time. They bulls****ed me that there wasn't but I figured it out."

Still, for all the little fights and the swearing—and Jack's as guilty as anyone else on that—he loves his sister and his parents, even if he does push things a bit. Being the youngest, and the only boy, he knows he can get away with a few things, and he makes sure he does whenever he can—staying out late, drinking, even some drugs—although half the time when he mentions things he's doing purely it's to test and push his parents' buttons.

HOW TO BE AN OZZY PARENT:

Your kids will test you a lot. Don't rise to the bait.

But while his friends complain about their parents, Jack knows his are cool—and while he might not admit it often, he knows he has a cool sister in Kelly. He'll come on tough, and perhaps overly cynical, but underneath he cares deeply for those closest to him. It's just that, like most teenage boys, he doesn't always show it on the surface. After all, you have to *seem* to be cool, as much as possible.

Growing up isn't easy for anyone, and like Kelly, Jack's had to do it in the public eye. But she's a girl, so there are things no one expects of her. He's Ozzy's son, the male offspring, and a lot of people probably expect him to be just like his father.

He's not, of course. He's very much his own person. The two do share several traits, however. Neither of them is very bothered about clothes (Jack wore the same clothes for about two years, and even now seems to throw on the first thing he can find). And they both have a wicked sense of humor, winding people up a bit, egging them along.

He still needs to learn some responsibility (just think about why he lost Lola), but that will come with time. And he's just a normal teenage boy in that he often thinks the world revolves around him. But he knows that for all the image of Ozzy, Jack's a part of what's really a perfectly normal family—they just swear a bit more than most people.

They can embarrass him. He understandably feels a little awkward when his mother flashes his friends, or when he sees his parents snogging—sex, after all, should be the province of the young. And he's at an age where public displays of affection by the family simply aren't cool.

HOW TO BE AN OZZY PARENT:

Don't be afraid to embarrass your children with affection. They'll get over it, and being loved is more important than being cool.

He can't understand why America has a love affair with the Osbournes, and he's not going to worry about it too much. He has enough to do, just being himself. There's still plenty of growing left.

Will he go on to college? Probably not. It seems more than likely that he'll go directly into the music business, probably working for his mother, and he won't need a college degree for that—neither of his parents have one, and they've managed just fine so far—better than most college graduates, really. And Jack isn't especially academic. He's home-schooled for just a few hours a day, enough to get by and earn a high school diploma when he's eighteen.

Still, he'll be okay. Both he and Kelly will. And it's not because they come from a family that's rock royalty (and also one of the funniest around). It's not even because there's plenty of money around—they like that, but they'll be expected to earn their keep. It's because of the love that's surrounded them as they've grown up. They'll have the time and opportunity to find themselves. Caring and loving can do more than a lot of people realize. Yes, Jack experiments, but so do many teenagers. He'll make up statistics to back up his claim. That's nothing new. He'll push his parents as far as he can, exasperate them at times, but like someone on a rubber band, he'll come bouncing back to them, because he loves them as much as they love him.

While Kelly might get annoyed by their parents going on at each other, asking them to shut up, Jack can just lie back and accept it. He can relax on the couch with his dad as easily as he can stay out at a club with his friends. And even if he's never touched a bat or a dove in his life, he's his father's son. And both Sharon and Ozzy are proud of him. And of Kelly and Aimee. They wouldn't want their children to be any way other than how they are.

Where Now?

The season's ended. The show's gone out on a high note. But no one can let it all go. It's been aired in Canada and is now being shown in the U.K.—although the May 19 debut of the show in Britain was delayed for unspecified "contractual reasons." Ozzy, Sharon, Kelly, and Jack have all become major media stars. Everyone wants them. Everyone wants to know their secret for being such a great family, as if there was something they could just tell everyone. They're the world's most functional dysfunctional family.

America loves Ozzy. Everyone loves Ozzy. He's been to dinner with the president of the United States, and at the beginning of June he performed by special request for Queen Elizabeth of the United Kingdom (although it's somehow hard to imagine her enjoying "Paranoid") at her celebration of fifty years as monarch. That's something Ozzy couldn't even have imagined a year ago. Back then he ruled his niche; these days he rules the media.

He's got the ratings and the money to prove it. MTV sent him a check for a quarter of a million dollars—a bit more than the

$20,000 per episode they promised. But then again, the ratings were a bit more than MTV had expected.

It's left everyone wanting more. And while the existing ten shows can be repackaged, endlessly rerun, put together in Ozzy marathons, and issued on DVD and VHS—all of which is likely to happen over the next several months—it's not the new material that everyone wants.

Season One is over. People are already clamoring for Season Two.

However, it's not quite that simple. The fame game has come into play. While they made $20,000 an episode for the first series, the figures bandied around for the next one are a lot higher—one report in the usually reliable *Daily Variety* stated that MTV could end up paying $20 million over two seasons to keep the Osbournes tied to the channel. But Sharon contended that the real figure was a lot lower than that, without giving any specific numbers. Both she and Kelly did say that a new deal had been reached with MTV. Interviewed on *Access Hollywood,* Kelly said, "I can't talk about [the money]. Not only do I think that it isn't anyone's business but I don't really like talking about it."

While the Osbournes seemed certain that a second season was a done deal, MTV wasn't quite as positive. A spokesperson from the network would only confirm that negotiations were going on, but said there was no deal in place yet. So who was right? Or was Sharon simply using some business strategy?

What seems almost certain is that there will be a second season. The show's too big to stop now. The demand's there, and it seems obvious that the Osbournes want to do it, for all the concerns they might have aired about the first and the problems of fame.

There will be changes the second time around, though. The biggest regret the family had was using their own house in Beverly Hills. It was too accessible to fans, and because they were people who went out in public, they themselves became too accessible. The main talk has been about using their farmhouse in England. And a rural Osbournes, living the country life, would make a complete change of pace, although whether it'll include Ozzy cleaning the barn or Kelly feeding the chickens remains to be seen (certainly after his last encounter with chickens in the 1970s, when he used a shotgun instead of feed). But, being more isolated, they're less likely to be mobbed by fans.

But, in fact, it will be mostly filmed, once again, in Los Angeles, according to MTV, which, on May 29, formally announced its new agreement for twenty new episodes of *The Osbournes* spread over two seasons, a deal Sharon called "absolutely f***ing amazing." Instead of the $20 million that had been bandied about, reports had it set at $5 million—still hardly chicken feed. And there would also be MTV specials on the Osbournes this summer, while Sharon had agreed to host a program on the Queen of England's Jubilee for VH1. Even Kelly was enjoying her fame, as her version of "Papa Don't Preach" became one of the most added songs to radio. The girl was a hit. And she had her chance to strut her stuff in front of millions when she performed the song on June 6 at the MTV Movie Awards.

So the family was continuing to do well, would stand to make a lot of money—especially if you added in merchandising. But so

THE TOP OZZY COLLECTIBLES (PRICES ON EBAY—MAY 2002)

1. Blizzard of Ozz, *signed by Ozzy, Randy Rhoads, and Bob Daisley, $510*

2. Blizzard of Ozz, *signed by Ozzy, $100*

3. *Diary of a Madman concert tour book, $90*

4. The Osbournes *crew itinerary, $90–150*

5. *Bark at the Moon tour shirt, $86*

6. *Blizzard of Ozz tour program, $75*

7. Ten Commandments *CD, $75*

8. No Rest for the Wicked, *signed by Ozzy, $61*

9. An Interview with Ozzy Osbourne, *7" picture disc, $61*

10. *Sealed box of Ozzy trading cards, $52*

would MTV, who, according to media sources, was selling thirty-second commercial spots on the new season for $100,000. Still, they'd earned it, after contract negotiations that (according to *The New York Times*) included frequently changing demands, such as a new house and lifetime psychotherapy for their pets. Finally, though, it was all signed and sealed.

Season One of *The Osbournes* had its revelations. But the biggest one came just after the tenth show had ended. In a cover story in *Blender,* Sharon asserted that Ozzy had been "p***ed for half the series. Generally, when you see him with his hair tied up on his head, he's p***ed."

So, for all the talk about him having cleaned up and being sober, Ozzy had reverted back to alcohol. He admitted that he'd tried AA and rehab, and it simply hadn't worked. This was the way he was, and you had to take him or leave him.

While Kelly didn't see the need to tell all that to the world, Sharon was supportive of her husband, and Jack didn't think that his father's drinking was a big deal; after all, it wasn't exactly anything new, was it?

But it was. Every indication had been that Ozzy was able to control his alcoholism, that he'd conquered it. And now, it appeared, he was exactly the same person he'd been many years before—just older, happier, and not biting the head off anything.

He was able to accept himself for who he was, and he'd finally come to terms with his drinking. To be sure, it wouldn't make his life any easier, but it had finally come into the open again, and perhaps that was a good thing. At least it didn't need to be a secret anymore. And it didn't affect the love everyone felt within the family.

HOW TO BE AN OZZY PARENT:

Be happy with yourself, and you can be happier for your family.

Maybe, now that he was a star, and in everyone's affections again, Ozzy didn't feel he needed to keep it quiet. The whole country had taken him to heart, and this revelation wasn't likely to change that. He was still a good father, one of the very best, and simply a cuddly person—not bad for a Prince of Darkness!

Really, no one even seemed to pick up on Sharon's admission about Ozzy, or even care about it. It was, well . . . just Ozzy being his wild and crazy self. However, it wasn't the only revelation to appear. In May 2002, the *Guardian* reported that Sharon and her father were now reconciled; they were speaking, at least, and Arden had finally met his grandchildren.

Drinking wasn't likely to affect Ozzy's singing; it never really had before. He'd consistently put on great shows when drinking. And he had a whole summer of them lined up with the Ozzfest tour, which was set to be bigger than ever, kicking off in Bristow, Virginia, on July 6, and finally coming to a halt on September 8 in Dallas. Predictions had a total of one million people coming to see it during those two months, quite an amount for twenty-four shows. But it would be Ozzy's new popularity that would drive things over the top. Yes, they had some big attractions for the younger crowd, like P.O.D. and System of a Down, but Ozzy would be the one wearing the crown, the headliner everyone would stick around to see—if only to just say they'd seen him. He'd reached that kind of stature now, a new plateau that would have seemed unthinkable for a heavy metal star aged fifty-three. But television can do odd things, and make superstars of the most unlikely people.

The big question is, can a second season of *The Osbournes* succeed and be as big as the first? If MTV pays out big money (and whether it's $20 million or less, you can bet the money's going to be big), they're gambling it can. And they'll do everything to make sure it is. Can there be the freshness and humor there was the first time around, though? Where everything was so natural, would it be possible to keep that for another season? Could the family remain unaware of the cameras and be themselves, without always thinking that they had to live up to the image they'd created? Or would they always be striving to be a little wackier, a little crazier?

Time will give us the answer, of course. At this point, plenty of people in America would love to see more of them. They're already bigger than wrestling (which is saying a lot), the hottest thing ever to emerge on cable. A second season will likely see viewing figures through the roof—and if Ozzy, Sharon, and the kids can just let their natural personalities flow, those figures will remain huge.

No one can fully predict what will be popular on television, of course. That's part of the fun of it all—and why we don't just have the same ten shows over and over. *The Osbournes* was the left-field hit of this season, for reasons the family themselves could never understand, but which we all can.

They make us happy, and feel better about ourselves. They put the fun in dysfunctional. Except, underneath all the weirdness and the language, they're far more functional as a family than most of us.

We laugh with them, at them, and at the situations that come up. But we learn from them, too. Who'd have thought you could learn to be a great father from a man who bit the head off a bat? Life is full of surprises, and *The Osbournes* has been one of the greatest. From a cult hero to instant superstar, and with the addition of a good parenting guide on the level of Dr. Spock.

Ozzy gives to a boomer generation proof that you can still be hip as you get older (hipper than ever, in fact, without becoming the kind of self-parody that Mick Jagger or Rod Stewart are), and that your kids can relate to you as a person, not just as a father. That's reassuring for a generation that's always seen itself as young, and is scared of growing older and grayer and out of touch.

But Ozzy's always broken the mold. He might wonder how long it can all go on—a question he's asked Sharon many times, but with no real answer—but it keeps getting better. It's as if, in middle age, he's been given the kind of Midas touch everyone desires. He has it all, the money, fame, the houses, the family, adulation, and the music. And he's done it all by being himself (and being guided by Sharon; no one could ask for a more devoted manager).

Is there anywhere else he can go from here? He's such a full-fledged celebrity that there's even been an hilarious short movie about him, *Being Ozzy Osbourne* (a parody of the underground hit *Being John Malkovitch*), in which an office worker finds that a shredding machine is a portal into Ozzy's mind. Ozzy is oblivious to the man being there, other than to complain about the new "third demon" in his head.

While he's not in the film himself, it's a definite tribute to a man who can be, well, off-center a lot of the time. Made before Ozzy's ascent to media darling, it's an interesting and funny homage.

And in addition to a film about him—at least, in a curious fashion—Ozzy has his own PlayStation video game, Dark Skies, which has been massively profitable. He's a brand now, as much as anything you'd buy in the grocery or department store. Very few rockers have managed that.

Quite where it can all end up can only be imagined. How much bigger can Ozzy get? Can he, in fact, even get any bigger than he is?

Really, there's nowhere left for him to go. His name is on the biggest traveling festival and one of the most successful events in musical history. His records sell in the millions. How do you top that? About the only way would be for the queen to give him an M.B.E., the same honor bestowed on the Beatles. And let's face it, with Ozzy's dubious track record, that's not exactly likely to happen anytime soon.

How long can he honestly go on in the business? At the moment, that's anyone's guess. He's fifty-three and still has all the energy and creativity he had thirty years ago. Fans still love him. There's no reason for him to stop, short of another illness. This is what he loves to do—it's the only thing he can do, really. And after retiring once, only to come back, he's in no hurry to do it again.

He'll probably spend less time on tour; there's no longer the need for him to be on the road eight months out of the year. Still, the road's in his blood right now, and he's not likely to quit, or even just limit his treks to Ozzfest. If he slowed down enough, he might just have to stop altogether!

He's certainly slowed down on making albums, but that's largely the way the music industry has changed. There's no longer the pressure to produce an album, or more, every year. Artists tour behind their albums for a lot longer, and when you have a huge catalog like Ozzy's, there's plenty of material to play in concert. A longer layoff between albums also means he can pick and choose his material, and wait for the best songs to mature for the next disc.

There was a long gap between his last two studio albums, although the new *Live at Budokan* is coming out quickly; but live albums have always been different, a filler or stop-gap. And it makes sense, with Ozzfest coming, and his popularity at an all-time high, to give fans new and old something they can buy. The odds are that the album will become one of his best-sellers ever.

And with a few new tracks, it gives him something fresh to play at Ozzfest. The interest in him will raise the energy level of the band, which will get the crowd higher—it'll be a rising spiral.

But it won't be the only Osbournes record on the market. There's also the *Osbourne Family Album,* out on Epic Records (the label for which Jack's a scout). That's the one with Kelly singing "Papa Don't Preach," joined by two members of Incubus. Originally Aimee was going to sing it; instead, she gifted it to her little sister. The definition of "family" would be fairly loose, as it extended to their former Malibu neighbor, Pat Boone, offering his version of Ozzy's "Crazy Train," and Ozzfest guest System of a Down covering Sabbath's "Snowblind." There will also be other, previously released material on the disc. Will it sell well? The show's been so hot that it's certain to just roar onto the charts, finding an audience far beyond the usual Ozzy fans. So what's on it? Here's the track listing:

"Crazy Train," Pat Boone

"Dreamer," Ozzy Osbourne

"Papa Don't Preach," Kelly Osbourne

"You Really Got Me," the Kinks

"Snowblind," System of a Down

"Imagine," John Lennon

"Drive," the Cars

"Good Souls," Starsailor

"Mirror Image," Dillusion

"Mama, I'm Coming Home," Ozzy Osbourne

"Wonderful Tonight," Eric Clapton

"Crazy Train," Ozzy Osbourne

"Family System," Chevelle

The show's success has also caused an increase in the price of Ozzy collectibles. While, as many retailers have said, he's been a solid seller for years, some have noticed a spike in demand, according to *Discoveries* magazine. The online auction site, eBay, has been doing a roaring business in Ozzy items, with more than twice as many listed as before the show began. Particularly hot, of course, has been anything connected with the show itself and the family. Quite a few people have been auctioning off Ozzy and Sharon's business cards, which have been going for as much as $15–25 each. The big prize, however, has to be crew itineraries for the show. As described by one seller on eBay, they are "complete wire-bound booklets used by the cast, producers, and crew of the MTV television series, *The Osbournes*. Includes lots of highly confidential and current info. How about the direct telephone numbers to the kids' rooms? Producer's office? Addresses?"

The odds are that it'll only take one call from an auction winner before those phone numbers are changed. In the meantime however, they've been selling for anywhere from $90 to $150.

Record company displays for the show have gone for as high as $62, and a trade ad for the series fetched $25. Even crew laminates are doing well, going for $25 each.

As if that weren't quite enough Ozzy, there's also a gallery in Maryland (The Game Face Gallery, PO Box 5820, Baltimore MD 21282-5820) that's offering a range of Ozzy porcelain figures. Seven-and-a-half inches high, and signed (but no price stated), they're selling well—as are the smaller, unsigned versions at $39). They even have porcelain Ozzy plates, signed in gold ink, and, again, smaller unsigned ones for $39.

So maybe it won't ever stop. Maybe Ozzy will keep rocking all the way to his grave. If he's lasted this long, given what he's done to his body, chances are he'll be around for quite a few years to come. And if he lives up to the reputation he established early in his career, he might even still be rocking from beyond the grave.

Even if he can't understand what makes him so popular with TV audiences, it doesn't matter. One thing Ozzy's learned in his years is how to accept. And he's taking this new-found celebrity in stride much more easily than his first flush of fame. He's learned how to pace himself and resist at least some of the temptations. The doves and the bats, it seems fair to say, are safe.

Ozzy on Disc

WITH BLACK SABBATH:

Black Sabbath (1970)

Paranoid (1971)

Master of Reality (1971)

Black Sabbath, Vol. 4 (1972)

Sabbath, Bloody Sabbath (1973)

Sabotage (1975)

We Sold Our Soul for Rock and Roll
(1976)

Technical Ecstasy (1976)

Never Say Die! (1978)

Reunion (1998)

SOLO:

Blizzard of Ozz (1980)

Diary of a Madman (1981)

Speak of the Devil (1982) Also known as
 Talk of the Devil

Bark at the Moon (1983)

The Other Side of Ozzy Osbourne (1984)

The Ultimate Sin (1986)

Tribute (1987)

No Rest for the Wicked (1989)

Ten Commandments (1990)

Just Say Ozzy (1990)

No More Tears (1991)

Live & Loud (1993)

Ozzmosis (1995)

The Ozzman Cometh: Greatest Hits
 (1997)

Ozzfest, Vol. 1: Live (1997)

Down to Earth (2001)

Osbourne Family Album (2002)

Live at Budokan (2002)

Ozzy on Video

Talk of the Devil (1982)

The Ultimate Ozzy (1986)

Wicked Videos (1988)

Sam Kinison Banned (1990)

Don't Blame Me (1991)

Alice Cooper: Prime Cuts (1991)

The Black Sabbath Story, Vol. 2 (1992)

Live & Loud (1993)

The History of Rock'n'Roll, Vol. 8 (1995)

Ozzfest 1: Live (1996)

Black Sabbath: The Last Supper (1999)

It's Only Rock'n'Roll (2000)

Satan's Top 40 (2001)

Adam Sandler Goes to Hell (2001)

Ozzy on Film

Wrestlemania II (1986)

Trick or Treat (1986)

The Decline and Fall of Western Civilization, Part II: The Metal Years (1988)

The Jerky Boys (1995)

In A Metal Mood (1996)

Howard Stern's Private Parts (1997)

Little Nicky (2000)

Lemmy (2000)

We Sold Our Souls for Rock'n'Roll (2001)

Moulin Rouge! (2001)

Austin Powers in Goldmember (2002)

Ozzy On-line

Perhaps surprisingly for someone of his stature and fame, there aren't hundreds of great Ozzy sites on the Net. You can catch him officially at www.ozzy.com, while all the information about *The Osbournes* can be found at www.mtv.com. Ozzfest is detailed at www.ozzfest.com, if you want to know what's happening there.

Great Ozzy fan sites are few and far between. The best by far is Ozzyhead (www.ozzyhead.com), which is as up-to-date and thorough as anyone could want. Past that you get into the not-so-current and the brief. So stick with the good stuff.

Acknowledgments

After beginning this book, I received the sad news that Mike Murtagh died, far too young, on May 2, 2000. So this goes out to him, too, a loyal friend and inveterate reader; you'll be missed by many people, mate. Linda and Graham were both incredibly supportive while I was writing, as they always are, making sure I had the time and space to complete the book on a tight deadline that got tighter. My mother, in England, offered constant words of encouragement. Thanks to Madeleine Morel, the best agent in the world, for the call back to action; to Tom Dunne, Pete Wolverton, and John Parsley at St. Martin's for their communication and suggestions.

While a book is written by one person, there are always plenty of others behind the scenes. Support came not only from family, but plenty of friends: Thom Atkinson (who's the author of a great rock'n'roll novel—check it out), Wally and Rina, Kevin, John Koenig at *Discoveries,* and others far too numerous to mention. Also, a special thanks to Dana and Kevan, who provided the endless supply of

Kerrang! magazines, a goldmine of information on Ozzy. Shame you didn't win anything this year; then again, neither did we. The lads and lasses of the Leeds United mailing list, who kept a boring season entertaining. And I'd be remiss if I didn't thank the makers of the very excellent Yorkshire Tea—their product kept me going all the way through the writing, as did walking with Brindle (who also offered constant companionship), and watching the antics of Zuni, Boodle, Mardi, Silvi, and Jess. Adam Hunter banged around upstairs and gave a neo-industrial soundtrack to the first part of the writing—but his results were spectacular. And thanks, too, to Ozzy, for being so entertaining for more than thirty years—very few can make that claim. I can still remember the thrill I had the first time I heard *Black Sabbath,* and the way it influenced the band I was in at the time.

The following articles were invaluable in the writing of this book: "Ozzy's Summer of Love," by Adrian Deevoy, in *Blender*; "Ozzy Osbourne," by David Gans; "Sharon Osbourne," by Ian Gittins, in *The Guardian*; "How to Manage like Sharon Osbourne," in *Fortune*; "Ozzy—Back Down to Earth," by Greg Sorrels; "Ozzy Osbourne," by Dave DiMartino, from launch.com; "Land of Ozz," by Ed Bark, from *The Dallas Morning News*; "The Osbournes, America's First Family," by Erik Hedegaard, in *Rolling Stone*; "Ozzy Osbourne: Tears of Satisfaction," by Deborah Russell, in *Billboard*; "Epic's Ozzy Osbourne Comes Down to Earth," by Wes Orshoski, in *Billboard*; "Osbourne Again," by Ken Tucker, in *Entertainment Weekly*; "All Aboard the Crazy Train," by Marc Peyser, in *Newsweek*; "Iron Maiden," from *Entertainment Weekly*; "At 53," by Greg Kot, *Knight-Ridder/Tribune News Service*; "American Goth," by Nancy

Miller and Evan Serpick, in *Entertainment Weekly*. Interviews with the Osbournes at mtv.com; "Black Sabbath: Out of the Blue, into the Black," by John Stix, in *Guitar for the Practicing Musician*; "The Great Southern Trendkill," by Steffan Chirazi, in *Kerrang!*; "Oh Come All Ye Faithful," by Joshua Sindell, in *Kerrang!*; "Ozzy Osbourne," by Joshua Sindell, in *Kerrang!*; "Prince of Darkness," by Paul Branningan, in *Kerrang!*; "Back in Black," by Phil Alexander, in *Kerrang!*; "The Godfathers," by Dave Everley, in *Kerrang!*; "The Last Supper?" by Phil Alexander, in *Kerrang!*; "The Last Word," by Sylvie Simmons, in *Kerrang!*; "Monsters of Rock," by Steffan Chirazi, in *Kerrang!*; "Talk of the Devil," by Liz Evans, in *Kerrang!*.